Recovering Addict: Addicted to Gangbangin'

DEWAN DENNIS

Published by A.D PUBLISHING, 2024.

RECOVERING ADDICT: ADDICTED TO GANGBANGIN'

First edition. May 6, 2024.

Copyright © 2024 DEWAN DENNIS.

ISBN: 979-8224463923

Written by DEWAN DENNIS.

Table of Contents

I wrote this book to serve as a teaching tool on how to rehabilitate gang members. The program I created and instituted, known as C.R.E.E.D, has already been proven to work. In reading this, you will learn about what causes a lot of the youth to become involved in gang-bangin' activity, living what I call the death style. We will get to the root of the problem: mental illness, more directly PTSD, and how it develops in our youths throughout the ghettos of America. I will lay out my method of treating it using my program known as C.R.E.E.D. with a lesson plan for you to follow and institute. In the end, you will read a testimony from someone who has already completed the C.R.E.E.D. program and turned from a life of gang-bangin'.

Along the way, you will hear commonly used terminology, and to help you understand the meaning of this terminology, I have included an urban dictionary that you may keep handy while reading to refer to. I want to thank you for purchasing and taking the time to read my book. It shows that you are concerned about this ongoing problem and are looking for a better solution to solve it. I believe with all my heart that C.R.E.E.D. is the absolute best solution to turn gang members away from the lifestyle once and for all. If you came here looking for my life story, I am sorry to disappoint you, but that is not what this is. It is about repairing our communities and fixing the growing problem that is tearing them down.

Urban Dictionary

Gang Bangin'- Participating in gang activity

Putin' In Work- Committing crimes for a gang

What's Crackin or **What's Popin**- "What's up"

Stackin'- To communicate with your hands

B-Walkin'- A dance performed by Blood members

C-Walkin'- A dance performed by Crip members

The Hood- Neighborhood or ghetto

Faction- Set of individuals that make up a gang

The Set- The gangs' turf or neighborhood or faction

Goon- A lunatic- addicted to puttin' in work

Out of bounds- To trespass in another gang's turf

Bein' on point- Highly focused, sharp

G-ride- Car

Chopper- An AK47 Assault riffle

G-Mackin- Hanging out

Let the Mossberg go- Shoot a Mossberg shotgun

Let the "chopper" rip- Shoot an AK47

Chirp Phone- Nextel phone's walkie-talkie feature

Jakes- Police

Heated- Upset

Sour D- A marijuana strain

Beef- Discord with other gangs' or individuals

Gunplay- The use of guns to settle a beef

Homie- Friend and or fellow gang member

Smoke- Kill/murder someone. "I'll smoke that fool."

The D- The city of Detroit

Chuckin the Deuce- Two-finger peace sign

The Dutch- Cigar stuffed with Marijuana

Local D-Boy- A neighborhood drug dealer

Gettin' Money- Making a lot of money

Hanging Up My Chucks

- Dewan Dennis

RECOVERING ADDICT ADDICTED TO GANG-BANGIN'

This book is dedicated to my deceased brothers:
Andre "AD" Dennis & Derek "Power" Dennis
It's hard pushing forward without you, but I will keep our family's legacy alive.
Until we all meet again, R.I.P.

Disclaimer: According to the author, this book will change the lives of people who are surrounded by gang culture and violence. To effectively address the problems caused by this unsightly illness, we must use a holistic approach.

The author also wishes to be very clear that the lessons he learned from the Gospel of Jesus Christ were what changed his life.

PROLOGUE

I have spent 19 years behind bars, 17 of those years in New Jersey State Prison. I've had the good fortune to serve the Christian community in several capacities since 2009, all of which have helped me deepen and broaden my understanding of Christianity.

As a minister, counsellor, and Bible teacher, I work with the prison ministry. I've been able to identify that many of the guys I've counselled suffer from PTSD (Post Traumatic Stress Disorder) because of my varied jobs within the church.

I lived a lifestyle that consisted solely of gang involvement for more than 20 years. Because of gang violence, I have lost a hundred friends and acquaintances.

When I was fifteen years old, I witnessed my stepfather fight cancer valiantly, just like a real soldier, and I also saw him lose his fight. During the same year, my brother was killed. I was shot twice in the head after that and ambushed more than once. I was shot at least fifty times, and throughout that time, I could literally feel and hear AR-15 rounds kissing and whistling past my face. Six concussions highlighted all of that, and I was soon diagnosed with PTSD, complex stress disorder, and traumatic brain damage.

THE DENNIS REPORT comprises a decade of research and 23 years of experience in what I call the "death culture." I didn't acquire this knowledge at Harvard, Yale, Princeton, or Brown. My course study comes from decades of living in the indelible slums of America. I've witnessed the loss of life via murder, gunfights, police brutality, and governmental manipulation. Having gang-banged for 23 years allows me·to speak the truth about these issues a little more than others.

These are years of study about urban warfare, PTSD, and the human brain under trauma. Here, I'll rely on a true story to relate the effects of trauma in the brain and how it negatively impacts a person's life. The names are fictitious, but the story is depressingly real.

A close friend of mine, we'11 call him Ray-Ray, grew up in Chicago's south side. It was a time when the murder rate had ballooned to nearly 700 homicides in a single year. Ray had been reared in foster care. He had lived in poverty and was already being abused by his foster parents by the time he turned twelve.

At 14, he had dropped out of school and ran away from his third foster home. That caused him to land in the waiting arms of the Bloods Street gang in the City of Newark, New Jersey. By 18, Ray was a full-fledged gang member whose name was already terrorizing the neighborhoods of Newark, Plainfield, Trenton, and Camden - 4 of the biggest cities in the state of New Jersey.

Gang-bangin' so fervently also brought about many vices for Ray, such as marijuana, alcohol, various prescription and illicit pills, and many other experimental drugs. I met Ray when he had just turned 28, and his dedication to gang life was much the same as a union laborer at a construction site. His frenetic and unpredictable behavior plainly displayed that he was suffering from mild schizophrenia and PTSD. Ray was not only a bad man but also in a terrible way, and soon the obvious and inevitable happened. After many years of activity in the gangbangin' culture, his terror had spanned 3,000 miles where he was convicted for a triple homicide in the state of California.

I haven't heard from Ray in more than 18 years, but sadly, I've heard about him. Not him per se, but several similar stories of other people with whom I had once run the streets. Ray's experience, along with the repeated pattern of so many like him, has spurred me to strive to gain a better understanding of the human brain, more specifically, how it is affected by trauma. This is how I have carefully constructed The Dennis Report.

Most gang bangers have experienced trauma in one way or another, more so if they've engaged in extreme violence. Complex stress festers within the body of any who lives under such conditions. During the early advent of PTSD, medical professionals believed that such trauma only existed in those who had once served in the military. We now know that PTSD can affect anyone who has experienced a traumatic event. Anyone engaged in warfare, urban warfare, anyone who has ever been tortured, assaulted, sexually assaulted, or anyone who has simply lost a fistfight while protecting his or her property - all these people can potentially face life-long, damaging· trauma.

According to the National Institute of Mental Health, not every traumatized person will develop full-blown or even minor symptoms of PTSD. Doctors have determined that symptoms of trauma must last for more than a month to be considered PTSD. It is also important to understand that some or all the symptoms can become chronic in some people.

Imagine a 5-year-old child being reared in a community where the· residents act like they are in a war zone, and the authorities treat the area like it is a war zone. That child is privy to the concept of people of color being destroyed by themselves and by law enforcement. What will become of this child? What will become of the millions of other children who· are experiencing the same thing? These children will soon turn into teenagers who adopt the concept of "me against the world."

For the most part, a child like this is being raised by their mother or possibly their grandparents. The father may have fallen victim to one of the "gorillas" or "monsters" that were put in place to haunt the urban community: crack, heroin, cocaine, LSD; PCP, ecstasy; alcohol... the monsters and their demons are endless. Or maybe the father, having no father of his own, abandoned the mother when the child was born. The bloodline suffers because it has no teacher that specializes in manhood.

It is communities (hoods) like these that have been failed by the local government and clergy. The black community has been strategically placed behind the eight ball. Anyone who understands billiards will know that the eight ball is off-limits in ·a game of pool. It is coveted and protected until all of the "stripes" and "solids" have been wiped out. You don't need a genius to tell you who the strips and solids are here.

People of color have overcome monumental obstacles of structural, institutional, educational, monetary, and medicinal racism. From the days of chattel slavery and Jim Crow laws to the 2020 killings of human beings like Breonna Taylor, George Floyd, and Ahmaud Arbery - it seems we've always been under attack by an institution that was designed for the destruction of people of color. Modern-day genocide all. Over again, manifesting itself through the lens of black-on-black violence. This, for our people, _ breeds nothing but trauma.

The entity of the black clergy was mentioned earlier. A large percentage of the black clergy seem content with packing pews to ensure that collection plates are stuffed. The black baby that cri.es out during the sermon is unimportant unless its mother has paid a tithe that she literally can't afford:

"it is the duty of every child of God to invest (spiritually) their life in the lives of those who are lost in darkness..."

Minorities have certainly fallen into the darkness of being_ spiritually and financially bankrupt. The great Dr. Martin Luther King fought to bring us out of this darkness and into a light that many of us have never seen. He did so with the threat of assassination looming over his head and the head of his family. He sacrificed many things, including his freedom, well-being, and ultimately his life, for the lives of millions. A gathering of supporters (Blacks and Hispanics) organized by the local 1199 Union of New York City listened to Dr. King explain what people of color must do...

"Now, what we have to do... is to attack the problem of poverty and really mobilize the forces of our country to have an all-out war against poverty... because what we have is not even a good skirmish against poverty. I-I need not remind you that poverty is the gap in our society, the gulfs between inordinate superfluous wealth · and abject deadening... poverty has brought about a great deal of despair, a great deal of tension, and a great deal of bitterness. We've seen this bitterness expressed over the last few summers in the explosions in our cities. And the great tragedy is that the nation. continues in its national policy to ignore the conditions that brought the riots or the rebellions into being. For, in the final analysis, the riot is the voice of the unheard. And what is it that America has failed to hear? It has failed to hear that the plight of the negro poor has worsened over the last few years. It has failed to hear that the promise of justice and freedom has not been met. It has failed to hear that large segments of white society are more ·concerned about tranquility and the status quo than about justice, humanity, and equality... and it is still true... it is still true that things are being ignored."

The bitterness, despair, and tension that Dr. King spoke about in 1968 still lingers largely amongst our people today, especially within the slums of America. The ugliness of then continues to rear its wicked head and is killing our communities by the hundreds.

Young men "and women our now packing America's prisons and filling the. country's graveyards. A designed deadly domino effect is destroying us. Strangely, the "us" is doing the killing. We are ruining ourselves through the culture of gang-banging, giving fuel to a fire that wishes to demonize and remove us from society altogether. The ·ones responsible for this plot are desperately hoping that we don't notice our circumstances because, in their minds, we don't care, so why should they? Why should they have sympathy for a monster?

This twisted rhetoric and trickery spills from the ill lips of people like retired professor John Dilulio. Back in 1995, Delusional, I mean Dilulio, referred to black troubled teens as "super predators." He said, "Our country is facing a huge threat from black boys who are godless and who can kill without any intelligible motive." Hillary R. Clinton blindly echoed the same senseless sentiment a year later.

She said, "We. must have an organized effort against gangs, just as in previous generations, we had an organized effort against the mob. We need to take these people on, and they are · often the kind of kids who are super predators with no conscience and no empathy. We can talk about why they ended up that way, but first, we must bring them to heal. I'm no longer dumbfounded by the idea that these two prominent people said such foolish things. I'm no longer confused why Hillary's first course of action was to punish instead of understanding why. She and Dilulio had no talk of inclusive humanity nor compassion.

These two and many others will never care to get to the root of the cause because it would expose the very government they serve. It would· detail how the controllers of this country have devised the destruction of people who· look like me. It would highlight how people of color are demonized. It would show how our issues are constantly front lined through every media outlet, which is not a bad thing unless government leaders are falsely controlling the narrative. What is the resounding result? Criminalize us in the eyes of everyone and then pack the prisons. The Department of Corrections is so overrun that the bars are starting to bend.

We need to ask ourselves about the life experiences of people like Ray. Have his experiences, along with the way society has treated him, made him more prone to violence? The answer lies within the science that governs mental health. Our children grow up in communities that greatly mimic war zones, and this has led scientists to study parts of the brain that control fear and stress. This certainly sounds like PTSD.

Doctors have paid close attention to the amygdala. These are paired almond-shaped structures located in the middle part of the brain. The amygdala has been associated clinically with a range of mental and emotional conditions. These emotions and conditions include depression, fear, and autism. A popular case discussed among physicians is one where a woman's amygdala is damaged, and she literally cannot experience the emotion of fear. The doctors have studied her extensively for research purposes and because a lack of fear is a trait that hinders adaptation. They conclude that this trait threatens the woman's survival and well-being.

Studies have shown that the pre-frontal cortex (where the amygdala is located) affects things like decision-making, problem-solving, and judgment. The pre-frontal cortex affects us in ways that we can't recognize easily. For example, when the pre-frontal area of the brain detects a controllable stressful situation, the amygdala is suppressed, which is an alarm system. When the amygdala is suppressed, so is one's fear. However, science proves that fearful memories will linger.

We should understand how PTSD is triggered may vary depending on individual genes. Neurologists have determined that things like childhood trauma, head injury, or mental illness have the potential to increase a person's risk by affecting the early growth and development of the brain. Another key factor is that such traumas can affect a person's ability to view things from a positive perspective.

Can this be the root? Is this the cause? Have we discovered why our young black men and women are killing each other like sport and play? Have we unearthed the truth as to why the prisons are overcrowded, and the graveyards are filled?

Some opine, me included, that gang banging is an addiction. Scientists have even developed detailed imagery of how addiction disrupts pathways and processes that lie beneath desire, habit, and pleasure. They now understand that addiction is possible without drugs. A recent study conducted by the Diagnostic and Statistical Manual of Mental Disorders has even shown evidence of behavioral addictions.

I've been debating numerous learned men and women for decades about the notion of addiction as it relates to gang banging. A recent Surgeon General's report has determined that addiction is a disease and not a moral failing. It is physical dependence, a compulsive repetition of an activity despite potential life-threatening consequences. If the report proves true, then how should we classify the compulsive repetition of gang banging, which without doubt, has life-threatening consequences?

Again, gang banging and all that it encompasses is an Addiction. The criminal justice system will never acknowledge such because society will view this as being soft on crime. That sounds political instead of medicinal, doesn't it? If the nation's scientists have determined that gang banging is an addiction or that it can become addicting, then such findings should be reflected within the laws of our government, should they not? _

Politicians combat this notion. They argue that gang members commit violence in every community. They understand the disdain that citizens have for gangs and their members. Many of them have been affected by gang violence in some way, so punishing a gang banger becomes a willful thing of ease. And the public never develops an understanding of why a person would ever indulge in such activity. The common person ignores science because the media portrays the ones who are addicted as monsters.

Experts in the field of mental health have long held that abuse victims - sexual, physical, emotional, or otherwise – are prone to grow up and offend others in the same way they were abused. This society has a duty to interrupt this deadly cycle of crime and violence. We need to "switch our pitch" as the baseball reference suggests and develop creative and holistic approaches to recognize PTSD and then treat it.

Ignoring the studies or failing to address this deadly dynamic will only aid this sad pattern of violence. Addicts will remain undiagnosed, there will be no treatment that would otherwise bring about change in their lives.

· Jon Grant, a psychiatrist from the Addictive Compulsive and Impulsive Disorders Clinic at the University of Chicago said, "Anything that is overly rewarding, anything that includes euphoria, or calming, can be addictive.

Now that we know and understand that addiction can exist without the presence of drugs, we can easily grasp the idea that gang-banging and all that it encompasses can qualify as an addiction. Our brains have a reward system when a person is addicted to drugs, the body craves drugs because the brain tells the body its reward is drugs. It's the same with anything else that the brain causes the body to crave.

The· brain has so many ways to reward the body, and all of those ways feed off of craving something. Cravings are driven by the neurotransmitter dopamine. Dopamine is· associated with every reward mechanism the brain has to offer. If something feels good to you, just know that dopamine is involved.

Gang banging, at least its sense of power and belonging, feels good. So good that it literally· distracts the gang member from understanding that he or she could be suffering from PTSD. This illness has already been proven that it can steer a person toward violent behavior. Gang culture creates a dependence, leading one to believe that they can't go through life without experiencing everything that gang life entails.

This dependence develops negative habits that allow a person to survive while engrossed in gang culture. The brain's reward system (fueled by dopamine} is triggered when a gang banger craves gang activity. When a gang member perceives a threat, he or she doesn't react like a normal person who has normal fear. (Remember the woman with the damaged amygdala?) Instead, a gang member will try to engage and eliminate a threat; at that moment, adrenaline soars, and dopamine floods the synapses. We've just described the same bodily function that happens during sex, gambling, eating chocolate, or anything perceived as pleasurable.

This process overwhelms the body's pleasure "hot spots." Now, a person will pursue a behavior, even if that action is guaranteed to produce negative results. The brain is making a person believe that those negative results are a reward.

I've personally witnessed how trauma affects the human brain. At the age of 15, I lost my stepfather due to cancer.

Months prior to his death, my brother was murdered. Years before losing these two most important people in my life, I was doing well in school and excelling in sports. That changed once I heard how my brother was left in the street next to a sewer drain; the left half of his head was blown off. The image was reawakened when the newspapers depicted him covered by a bloody white sheet on the front page.

I snapped. Instantly. I went from a well-mannered 15-yearold football star to ruthlessly bitter gangster seemingly overnight.

The trauma didn't stop there. You already know that I've witnessed the murder of some of my closest friends. I've been shot on two occasions, neither of them pleasant. I've suffered six concussions. Pretty much 23 continuous years of my life are filled with tragedy.

I was diagnosed in 2019 with T.B.I. (traumatic brain injury). Several CT scans were conducted on my brain; a neurologist concluded rather quickly. It _wasn't until 2021 that I began to feel like I was breaking free from the yoke of mental 'illness. My conviction about this issue is firm, and I'm certain that those who live in these war-torn communities also suffer from PTSD. There is help to fight PTSD for our heroes who defend the democracy of these American shores, but there is no help for some of the people who simply live within these shores. Why is that? Soldiers aren't the only ones suffering from trauma.

If the symptoms of PTSD cause a person to pursue ill-advised behavior, regardless of noticeable consequences, then there needs to be a re-examination of those who enter our criminal justice system. This is important because of the case law that governs men's rea (criminal intent). What was the thought process, even while knowing that a particular act is illegal?

If a murder is plotted and carried out, this is considered a first-degree homicide. What would it be considered if the mindset of the individual who committed the crime was altered due to PTSD? Is it still a first-degree offense? Remember, PTSD affects the way we think. The pre-frontal cortex affects our decision-making, problem-solving, and judgment. This sounds an awful lot like the elements that qualify a guilty verdict for first-degree murder.

The crux of the criminal statute for first-degree murder focuses on a person's state of mind. So, what is the mind state of a person who has· been diagnosed with this dangerous mental illness?

Shouldn't our criminal justice· system allow this person's diagnosis to influence how he or she is sentenced? The answer is yes, even if this person is a gang member, or rather, should I say, especially if this person is a gang member.

I know some will ask, "Why spend tax dollars on mental health treatment for gangbangers? "The gangbangers are the ones terrorizing our communities." Those who hold this sentiment must understand that a moral duty is upon us to help ALL- of humanity, even those who may not deserve it.

This country is filled with packed prisons, largely because we have failed to provide healing for those who may be suffering from an illness that makes people prone to violence. Tax dollars are doled, shifted, and manipulated in ways that a normal citizen may never understand. Why can't these tax dollars be used to bring healing to mental illness patients, whether they are soldiers, football players, construction workers, doctors, or even a gang banger? It can't simply be the criminal aspect of things because there are plenty of soldiers who are criminals. Plenty of football players tackled their girlfriends instead of running backs. Plenty of construction workers used their hammers to hit something other than nails.

Your tax dollars are already being spent on every prisoner in every prison in every state, so the argument of "my money isn't for the gang-banger" is a weak argument. Your money clothes all prisoners, feeds all prisoners, houses all prisoners, and provides medical treatment for all prisoners. Is it not wiser to direct your tax dollars toward attacking something that can cause a person to commit a crime? I say it is wiser, but certain people in control know that packing their prisons means packing their pockets... with your tax dollars.

It is imperative that our legislators enact more laws that focus on helping people and not just punishing them. Three decades of a misguided criminal system has taught us that being "tough on crime" is not the answer. We must take a different, smarter approach to reforming crime and punishment, especially when considering those diagnosed with PTSD.

Allowing this science into the courtroom is not far-fetched. A few years ago, our criminal justice system changed· the way juveniles can be sentenced. In Miller v. Alabama [567 US 460, 132 Set. 2455, 183 L Ed 2d 407 (2012) J, the court held that· imposition of mandatory life terms for children under the age of 18 violated the Eighth Amendment of the U.S. Constitution, sighting it was "cruel and unusual" punishment.

Part of the court's holding mentioned that when a juvenile is sentenced, the child's "diminished moral culpability" and "mitigating qualities of youth" must be heavily considered. These mitigating_ qualities include:

...chronological age and its hallmark features- among them: immaturity, impetuosity, failure to appreciate risk and consequences, and the family and home environment that surrounds them...

Imagine a home from which a child is unable to extricate himself, no matter how brutal or dysfunctional.

Brain science is the reason the law regarding juvenile sentencing guidelines was changed. Science shows that a young person's brain is not fully developed. Putting deference aside, modern science supports the commonsense notion that 18- to 20-year-old tend to be more impulsive than their slightly older counterparts. See, e.g., Brief for the Am. Med. Assn. et al. Amici Curiae in Support of Neither Party Miller v. Alabama·.

Earlier, we mentioned some of the areas of the brain and their function. Here's what the experts say:

"The brain's frontal lobes are still structurally immature well into late adolescence, and the prefrontal cortex is one of the last brain regions to mature. This, in turn, means that response inhibition, emotional regulation, planning and organization... continue to develop between adolescence and young adulthood..." (citations omitted); Lawrence Seinberg et al, Age Difference in Future Orientation and Delay Discounting, 80 Child Dev.28,40-41 (2009) [(C)]... "hangs in impulse control and planning are mediated by a cognitive control network... which matures more gradually and over a longer period into early adulthood." NRA, Inc.V. Bureau of Alcohol, Tobacco, Firearms, and Explosives, U.S. Court of Appeals for the Fifth Circuit, 700 F.3d 185.

The same laws in Miller v. Alabama can surely be applied to those who suffer from PTSD, specifically the "mitigating qualities." Poor decision-making, behavior control, overreacting, abandonment issues, family history, depression, and violent outbursts the root of these things should be examined· and cured.

Our New Jersey Supreme Court has detailed the science of· PTSD in Burnell v. Wildwood Crest Police ·Department, 176 NJ 225, 240-41, 822 A.2d 576 (2003), beginning with its characterization in the late nineteenth century as "hysteria," and the notion of traumatically induced mental disorders is nothing new. A diagnosis of PTSD can cover a broad variety of stresses and symptoms and may result from a single traumatic event, such as a car accident or continued exposure.to traumatic events, such as domestic abuse or trauma that occurs from being engaged in combat.

PTSD is recognized in case law to some degree. Courts in Colorado, Maryland, North Carolina, and Virginia have concluded that, depending on the facts, PTSD may either be an occupational disease or an accidental injury. Generally, each of these cases found PTSD to be an occupational disease when developed over time from multiple stressors unique to a person's employment. These cases aptly apply to the situation presented in these writings. Nothing inherently exists within a PTSD diagnosis, depending upon the facts, that would preclude its treatment either as accidental injury or occupational disease.

Since its initial application to combat trauma, large-scale diagnoses of PTSD have been made in cases of survivors of domestic violence· and childhood and sexual abuse. The· same case has been made for persons seeking asylum because of. Political violence or torture. The same goes for those who survive natural disasters. Most recently, many of the rescue workers and first responders during· the horrific 9/11 incident of 2001 have been diagnosed with PTSD.

Notice that the NIMH (National Institute of Mental Health) did not mention anything about urban violence. As mentioned earlier, doing so would be considered too soft on crime.

Well, the NIMH is a government-funded entity. I guess hip hop artist JayZ said it best, "Politics as usual." Policy, not politics, should be established fairly when governing people's lives. If not, things get very dangerous.

Getting back to being government-funded, I recall _a report I read in the FCN paper. It was reported that in 1970 our government funded what two

Harvard professors knew as the Boston Project. Doctors Stanley Walzer and Park Gerald conducted a study on chromosome screening in a predominantly black Roxbury section of Boston. Male newborn babies were screened for the XYY genetic signature, which was already proven to be a white genetic signature. In this study, nurses distorted the test results of the fetuses by falsely reporting a positive result.

Those same nurses also encouraged expecting mothers to abort their male babies, saying that their child would grow up to be a violent sexual predator because of the XYY chromosome. They were saying that these black boys would grow up to· be literal menaces to society. It's important to know that this study spanned ten years, all funded by the Unites States government.

I don't hold my breath believing that this government will consider urban warfare (gang-banging) an addiction that can lead to a diagnosis of PTSD. Time hasn't changed, just the. People exist within time, and the attack on black men is still prevalent. We can't change time, but we can certainly change the laws. Our first course of action should be to get the law to recognize that gang members are who they are largely because of trauma, mental health issues, and particularly PTSD and its symptoms.

In New Jersey, this issue is governed by N.J.A.C. SA: 6-2.1 which states: The New Jersey Post Traumatic Stress Disorder/Readjustment Counseling Program (PTSD/R) was established to assist in the form of clinical counseling, and continuity of care to veterans discharged from other than dishonorably from the <u>Armed Forces of the. United States</u> and their families. The New Jersey program is intended as a supplement to similar United States Department of Veterans Affairs or other government-sponsored programs, or when such assistance is exhausted (in New Jersey, PTSD must be determined in an Administrative Law system, ruled upon by a judge).

Our government has funded mental health programs to treat our war veterans, and that treatment is well-deserved and well earned, but what about giving that same treatment to people who are not part of the Armed Forces?

If a person has a history of mental health issues, this should be presented to the courts as a mitigating factor prior to sentencing. This is not ·to say that one should escape the punishment for his or her crime, but rather that one's. mental health must certainly be a factor, especially pertaining to PTSD. In fact, the mental health of a person should be reflected in the early stages of any criminal proceeding within the pre-sentencing report.

Chapter 10 of this book includes the C.R.E.E.D. program.

This curriculum is intended to be a government-funded program that will provide gang members with proper treatment and therapeutic help. This program be instituted in all county jails, prisons, juvenile facilities, and ·halfway houses.

CREED should be established in every state throughout this country.

"Each generation must discover its mission, fulfill it or betray it, in relative opacity."
-Frantz Fanon

A special shout out to:

My mother, who has been by my side from day one as I continue to fight this wrongful conviction for the past 19 years. Mom, you are my rock!

My friend....**101thegreat**. You've been here holding me up for 19 years. I salute you, brother. Not only have you been there for me, but you've raised my son. You took over for me as a father ever since these chains of incarceration were wrongfully placed on my feet and hands. I love you, man. ·

Introduction

I was addicted to death - I'm now a recovering addict, but I was addicted, nonetheless. My drug of choice? Gang-bangin'. This way of death (it can't be considered a way of life) has such a strong hold on so many of the world's great thinkers- mothers, fathers, the girl next door, the boy with the paper route, or the mechanic that fixes your car. From the high school dropout, who eked his way through the police academy to the thug on the corner with his pants drooping below his ass, and even the well-dressed entrepreneur with the inviting smile, "gang-hangers" surround you and me like the air we breathe.

Ha, ha. I laugh because it was told to me when I was a child that children are the future. If this proves to be true, then we are seemingly waiting for a future that shall never come. I say this because, as I once was, the young people of today are addicted to death, and they don't have the wherewithal to deal with it. Their fetish with death must be treated like any other addiction, and the youth, along with the ones responsible for them, must come to realize that gang-bangin' is a fast-paced epidemic. And it will not slow down until this disease is cured, one symptom at a time... one person at a time. I've done the research because I've lived the research, and I've made myself the first test subject to the theory of "The Recovering Addict".

Fighting against my cure are criminologists and politicians who like to advance the thought of "getting tough on crime." Ha, ha - I laugh again because this notion is such a bunch of nonsense. Forty-four thousand dollars a year - do you know what that figure represents? That is the individual amount paid toward The Department of Corrections by every taxpayer in the United States. These dollars are used to house, feed, clothe, and medicinally care for the two-point-two million incarcerated persons throughout America. The problem with the forty-four thousand is that it is being used to fuel addiction instead of fighting against it. I stopped asking myself why more people walk in and out of the doors of prisons than they do the doors of college campuses. I stopped asking myself why the police presence grew five times over in the ghettos of America during election time. I stopped asking myself these questions because the answers always seem to lead back to one underlying factor - our children are still dying because they remain addicted to death. They will continue to do so until they, as well as the ones responsible for them, realize that we are failing to restore life to a dead generation. Why did I decide· to write this book? It's quite simple; _ in fact; I've already clued you as to why... I, too, was addicted to death, And because of my addiction and others like me, our youths are finding themselves inundated by a modern-day genocide. Asking for this problem to be fixed is futile if I am a part of the problem myself. I, too, was one of the misguided. I created more havoc in my community than a storm can create rain drops. For over twenty-two years, I was addicted to the "death-style" of gangs. I know why a young person chases the dream of becoming the next Al. Capone. I know why the biggest dope dealer America has ever seen is being fashioned at this very moment. I know why the leading· cause of death in the inner-cities is murder. I know why a person can spend half of his or her life in prison, then rejoin society and be swooped up by the same addictions over and over. I also know that if the words "tough on crime" continue to be heralded instead of "smart on crime", then the solution to the addiction of gang-bangin' will elude us all like a black ant on a black rock in the black of the night. I know all these things, and if I don't teach them to you, sooner or later, it will be your child, your family member... or you, who· will be unexpectedly making their way to the coroner's office. or to the "big house" all because of an untreated addiction... gang-bangin'!

* * * * *

Gang Bangin' had us addicted like it was a Newport.
-The Game

Chapter 1
The Addiction

Chapter 1
The Addiction

The average person knows and understands what an addiction is and what it can do to a person. For those who are not so average will come to realize the seriousness and the commonness of an addiction over the next few pages.

Have you ever seen a person who was addicted to some sort of narcotic? I don't know why I asked the question because I know you have. Even if you claim to have never seen anyone use a drug in your entire life, you have most definitely witnessed the ill- effects that drugs can cause. The girl at your office who continuously shows up to work late and scurries off to the bathroom every twenty minutes probably has a one hundred dollar-a-day habit. She tells you it's from her weak bladder, and you believe her until you read the paper and find out that her body was discovered in a part of town where she had no business being. The teacher at your kid's school that everybody likes - he uses numerous drugs so teenage-girls can think he's cool. You have no idea about him either until you find a text message or an e-mail on your fifteen-year-old daughter's computer saying that he enjoyed their time together last night. And what about you? You may not be addicted to heroin or acid, but there's something that you've convinced yourself you can't live without: the morning cup of coffee that often replaces breakfast, the morning cigarette that gets smoked before the teeth get brushed, the sexual gratification that forces married couples to betray trusts; the diabetic who gulps down gallons of Butter Pecan, even though he or she knows the sugar is going to end their life. The truth of the matter is addictions exist - the apparent and the not-so-apparent, and they have worked their way to becoming commonplace.

The gang-banger's addiction to the "death style" has become commonplace as well. I don't have to rely on secondhand information because I've witnessed it for most of my life. I've seen my old comrades (most of whom are dead or serving life in prison) willingly engage in gun battles under the brightness of daylight. The high of the "death style" makes them believe that they can encounter an army of twenty or more and walk away unscathed. In that instant, the gangbanger misplaces reality and adopts the mindset of a racehorse with blinders on. There is no stopping until that racehorse forages his or her way across the finish line, and therein lies the problem. For the gang-bangin' racehorse, there is no finish line! There is no trophy, no ribbon, no reward; all that lies in wait is another gun battle or the grave. Subsequently, this has become an addiction of commonplace for anyone who lives this sort of "death style." The gangbangers refer to it as "puttin' in work." Fear- very much like reality - no longer exists because a gangbanger cannot eat, he cannot sleep, he cannot survive until he "puts that work in." It is attacking your enemy when they least expect it, it's the killing of the five-year-old girl, who was jumping rope on her front porch when a bullet intended for your enemy removed her from this world. It is the couple who was shot execution-style because they were out for ice cream and, while on a stroll, witnessed something that they shouldn't have. "Puttin' in work" is going after your adversary because they are in the wrong neighborhood, wearing the wrong colors at the wrong time of day. Oh, and don't you dare be appalled by the bluntness of my words; this explanation of addiction needs to be up front and in your face. There is a reason doctors use the term "blunt force trauma." Blunt force is the repeated beating (usually to the head) with an open hand, fist, or some sort of hand-held object. Most gangbangers beat harm into a person; beat a message into your mind. Most gangbangers beat harm into a person; I'm using the same tactics to beat a message into your mind.

I want to start with some statistics: in 2009, Chicago, Illinois, suffered 458 homicides. That's 458 autopsies, 458 funerals, 458 obituaries, 458 grieving families, and 458 occasions when all of us didn't recognize that our nation was undergoing a modern-day genocide. Do you think Chicago was the only city that attempted to murder itself? What about St. Louis, Missouri; Newark, New Jersey; Camden, New Jersey; Dayton, Ohio? I could name at least fifteen more cities in California, all of which have had enough recent homicides (in my opinion) to place the United States under a state of emergency.

Most of these homicides are being committed by children, some no older than fifteen. Now, do you understand why I laugh when people say that children are our future? I don't laugh because I think it's funny; I laugh to keep myself from crying. We must start giving credence to the sicknesses that our young people are facing, not the physical ones that doctors work tirelessly to cure, but the mental ones... the addictions.

"The ghetto" is swarmed with addiction - so much so that the effects of gang-bangin' have spilled over into middle-class suburbia. The places where businesses are supposed to thrive, and families are supposed to flourish have turned into actual war zones. A tenth grader will wake up one day and decide he wants to blow up his school. A young mother may decide that her two-month-old baby is not worth the trouble and smother it in its sleep. This destructive behavior comes from somewhere, and it's usually due to a person being deprived of a thing they are so greatly addicted to. Let's look at something: when a drug addict is undergoing withdrawals, he or she experiences painful mental and physical breakdowns. That person is usually isolated and sedated-sometimes physically restrained. They are literally forced to deal with their addiction head-on, but there are places for them to go and people to help them.

Not only can a gang-banger be addicted to drugs or alcohol and not even know it, but he or she couples this addiction with the "death style." The gang-bangers only recourse is to manifest his addiction through violence. Unlike the drug addict, a person addicted to "puttin' in work" is not going to find a rehabilitation center that specializes in his or her addiction. They are left to deal with this problem on their own; and their way of dealing with it adds to the statistics of homicide mentioned earlier in this chapter.

What are we to do? Firstly, all of us need to wake up whether we are the victim or the victimizer. The victimizers (the gang-bangers) believe that there is some great prize waiting for them at the top of the "kill-chain". While they lie in a coma after being shot, they still hold onto thoughts of delusion. Even in prison or jail, they continue to fester in their minds the idea of getting out and getting back on top. Some don't even wait to get out of prison. They put their murderous talents to use while they are inside the walls of confinement; for them, prison has become a training ground. On the other side of the coin, the victims seem to think that prison is the only answer, the only recourse, the only cure to such an addiction. As gang-bangers well know, prison is a hardened place. It is a place fashioned out of iron, concrete, and steel. Its caretakers are improperly trained, and its inhabitants have no choice but to become hardened like the walls and bars that surround them.

The penitentiary is no longer a place for the penitent. It used to be a place where rehabilitation was the loudest roar in the jungle. Then, someone had the keen insight to see that recidivism was going to be a problem, but that same someone didn't have the common sense to deal with it properly. Now we have a prison system that generates billions of dollars, and the men and women pulling the strings realize that to keep the dollars flowing... people are going to have to be kept in prison. This is where rehabilitation has been forced to take a back seat.

In the year (2011), New Jersey legislature passed a bill that will award an incarcerated person an opportunity to be released from prison six months earlier than originally intended. Governor Christie repealed this same bill because it was alleged that two persons released under the stipulations of the "Six Month Early Release Act" violated the terms by committing more violent crimes. The assembly woman behind the bill, Ms. Bonnie Watson-Coleman, has been hammered by Christie and his supporters, all because the assemblywoman saw fit to attempt to bring change to an ever-failing penal system. I have to say that in no way is this the assembly woman's fault. If a person is released from prison six months earlier than expected and he or she runs off and kills someone, please believe they would have killed six months ago or six months later, for that matter. The question we should be asking is, "What happened to that person during their incarceration?"

If a person commits a crime, I am all for them paying the price... I'm all for them giving back to the society that they have taken from. I'm also all for finding out what is wrong with such a person. How else are we to correct, prevent, and rehabilitate?

For those who don't want out of the "death style", prison or the life which you serve (death) is waiting for you. For those who are seeking to get out, I believe this book will shed light upon a dark and grim situation-a situation where 44% of African Americans and 18.4% of Latinos continuously display aggression toward themselves and authority. I wonder what would be the results if I rounded up every gang-banger in America and gave him or her a CAT scan? Or what if they were all given some sort of psychological examination? Am I too much of an optimist to say that an underlining commonality would be discovered? Chicago had 458 homicides in 2011; Philadelphia had over 200 murders in the same year; Compton, Watts, Detroit... the list goes on. Many of these murders were committed by persons between the ages of 14 and 25. What does this tell me? One-these are mid-eighties/late-nineties babies we're talking about here. Two born during an era when crack cocaine was their mother, father, teacher, and friend. Most of them were born addicted to crack-cocaine. If they were born with an addiction, then it is only plausible to assume that most of their choices in life will lead to other addictions.

Scientists have proven that a person born while addicted to a drug has what the medical world refers to as "dark spots" on their brains. Can these "dark spots" impact a person's thinking? These same "dark spots" have been mentioned in many studies regarding TBI (Traumatic Brain Injury). When a soldier is diagnosed with TBI, which often triggers PTSD, psychologists say they become more prone to acts of suicide. So, if it is proven that a gang-banger suffers from TBI or PTSD, should they be awarded the same psychological treatment as that of the soldiers of war? Let's face it...gang-bangin' or the "death style"... it's nothing but a violent and destructive way of committing suicide.

* * * * *

Chapter 2
Why is My Loved One in a Gang?

"Must everyone live in fear that every word he speaks may be transmitted or recorded and later repeated to the entire world? I can imagine nothing that has a more chilling effect on people speaking their minds."
      -Supreme Court Justice William 0. Douglas

Chapter 2:
Why is My Loved One in a Gang?

There are so many concerned parents and loved ones who are struggling with this question. Of the hundreds and thousands of fathers and mothers, aunts and uncles, and grandparents, many seem to think that they are the ones who have done something wrong. Have you ever heard one of your parents say, "Boy, I raised you better than that!"? Here's a famous one, "I don't know where I went wrong with you!" The child, after hearing statements like this for most of his or her young life, begins to break the innate connection between a mother and her son or a father and his daughter. This supports the notion that many so-called gang experts purport; they say that gang members join these gangs in a frantic search for acceptance or that they can feel a sense of belonging to something. I can't argue with this rationale, but if we truly want to begin to cure this sickness, we must dig deeper than simply asking why our son or daughter joined a gang-we need to ask ourselves what possible reasons caused them to stay.

The so-called experts say there are many reasons why a young person would join/stay in a gang. Among them are our young ones who are looking for a role model, or they are looking to find a place of acceptance. This was true ten years ago; however, things have changed. In fact, the only thing that is guaranteed to all human beings in existence is change. As the night changes into the day, so does the young change into the old. The very essence of a person (the cells) is constantly changing. In ten years' time, a human being will replace every single cell in his or her body; this means that he or she has become a completely new person. After years of changing themselves, the cells weaken and become filled with less vitality, which leads to life-changing into death. And these so-called experts (I refer to the experts of gang warfare as "so-called" because one must first live and breathe a thing before one can consider himself an expert) have no idea how to adopt the mindset of a gangbanger. Quite simply, it is too dangerous for them. Why do you think that some of the most successful police officers are also at the top of the list of the world's most sophisticated criminals? The government employs criminals all the time because the wicked-minded know how to stop the wicked-minded. I am in no way detracting from the years of study that a person must undergo to understand the human brain. However, it must be said that no sociologist or psychologist can truly understand the mind of a full-fledged gang-banger unless they have picked up a gangster's flag and adopted everything that comes along with it-the acceptance, the initiation, putting in work (the first step toward the addiction), the violence, the sense of power; until all of these things course through a person's veins, their understanding of gang-bangin' will remain limited at best. Even with all my experience in the "death-style", there are some questions that I still can't answer. For example: why, oh why on this seemingly God-forsaken earth, where the night turns into day, and the day into night, where the heavens battle with hell, and wrong combats right, why, oh why does mankind find the need to want to kill themselves off willingly? This is not a far-fetched question. People, quite frequently, engage in things that may kill them. Drugs, for instance, have already been mentioned as one of the many things that will urge a person-toward death. Cigarettes-it says in plain language on the package that the product will kill you. Alcohol-a person knows the ill effects of overindulging in liquor, yet more people drive inebriated than they do straight nowadays. People purchase handguns without the proper training. Even with all the diseases, people still frolic from fling to fling without protecting themselves. Bungee-jumping, paragliding, snake charming, alligator and bear wrestling the truth is... danger excites us!

The adrenalin begins to surge, the endorphins explode, our senses are heightened, and, along with them, our sexuality. These chemical reactions of the body convince the mind that we are invincible, indestructible, and immortal, yet we fail to understand the concept of change. As mentioned earlier, the young shall turn into the old, which means life will become death. It is guaranteed and coming for all of us; still, the gang-banger chases after death like a "john" chases a hooker., like a nymphomaniac chase after the immediate gratification of sex, like a "wino" chases Johnny Walker Black. A gang-banger chases after death like a dope-fiend seeks and pursues dope. Now, tell me if gang-bangin' is an addiction or not!

Gang-bangin' used to care about color. It still does in some respects- some get down with the blue, others with the red. Some get down with the black and gold. There is almost a color for everything, but the color I speak of is the color one cannot change: the color of one's skin. My Black and Latino brothers and sisters enlisted in so many gangs during the late eighties and early nineties. It just appeared to be the right thing to do for a person of color. Now? Now you see white people, Indian people, Arab people... people from any nation anywhere joining gangs. With this being the case, why does one only find the Blacks and Latinos doing most of the killing? Why are most of the killings being done not only by them but by themselves?

Before I go further, something needs to be made clear. I do not believe that it is the gangs themselves that created this destructive way of thinking. Gang activity fuels the fire, but human hostility toward fellow man has existed since the earliest recollections of time. There is a common saying among well-trained martial artists "The first cave man picked up a rock and hurled it at the other caveman; the message was clear... survive!" It seems to be embedded in the human soul that we must always be better, bigger, or bolder. We take, take, take, and win, win, win at all costs until there is nothing left to conquer. In doing this, we fail to realize that the more we take and the more we win, the more someone else is missing out or losing. No one, absolutely no one, wishes to don the title of "the loser." This is true in our places of business, in our social lives, even in our homes, so, we begin to take, and we try to win. The father takes from the mother by hiding his wine bottles, or he conceals one of his other dangerous vices, while the mother takes from the father by misusing his earnings, or she simply supports her husband in wrongdoing by keeping silent. The parents also take from each other by trying to outdo his or her counterparts regarding raising the children. The children take from each other because they watch their parents, and they see that one sibling is being favored over the other.

This behavioral pattern is more prone to happen within the household of minorities. How so? The family will take, take, take until its sense of identity is taken away. Our Black and Latino brothers and sisters have no idea who they are anymore, and since the number of minorities is vast and many in this country, the children of other races want to join in right along with them. They mingle with each other at school or other places of common ground, and they infest themselves, spreading this infestation into everything around them. The danger of it all is that the infestation remains hidden until it is too late, it's like finding a cancerous lump that is too far developed within the body. We need to seize hold of our children before the lump has a chance to develop its deep rooting.

The reason why cancer spreads so quickly within the body is because it appears new and attractive to healthy cells. They start to mimic the sickness and want to be like the infestation, while the few cells that try to fight off the disease are overpowered, pushed around, and bullied into a silent corner. The infested cells realize that there is strength in numbers, and they begin to multiply and outnumber everything, taking complete control. The cells attract and develop more cells that look and think just like them, and they destroy everything else! And this, by use of the basic building block of the human body (the cell), is how a gang is formed.

I'm tired of telling people to educate our children, but there's no other way to look at this debacle. Education has become nothing but a catch phrase. If you send them off to school, the young people are taught about Christopher Columbus (whose story is one of the biggest lies in existence). They are taught about America... America, of all places! A place in which history started in a state of death and treachery (slavery) and thrived off the notion of take, take, take! As we breathe in America's scenery these days, we see that the economy is "shot to shit," and China owns everything that we have. Our products are overpriced, the people are overworked and overtaxed, and if that's not bad enough, they are highly underpaid. I wish not to venture off into a political spill, but if things don't start to change, the school systems will end up ashamed to teach our children the grand tales of this overrated land of ours. America began foraging its path while, at the same time, leaving a trail of destruction; if we can't change its course before the cancer takes complete control, then we must change the course of its people-starting with the children.

Ah-ha! There is that word "change" again. What if our children don't want to change? Are we to pass them by? Leave them to the scavengers on the side of the road? That would certainly be easier than trying to re-teach the youth about themselves. The sad reality is that all the preaching and teaching in the world is not going to make a bit of difference if our youth of today do not want to change themselves. While they are struggling to figure things out, the people who know better (you and me) cannot abandon them. If we do, there is an OG or a Big Homie waiting around the corner whose sole purpose is to fill that void of abandonment.

It used to baffle me how a well-educated person with all sorts of grandiose degrees could not capture the minds of children in a classroom, yet a gang member-one who could barely speak the English language was able to not only teach a child but provide that child with a sense of confidence! A person isn't born with hate or malice in his/her heart; these are learned behaviors, and we need to learn how to make this dangerous behavior less attractive to our youths.

I'd like to go back a bit and talk more about these so-called gang experts. I have a lot of experience with gangs, more than most, but you have yet to hear me refer to myself as an expert. I can't; I've already told you that I am a recovering addict. Now, if I can't label myself an expert, what makes someone else think that they can? There are no experts in this thing; often, the so-called experts of gang warfare are misinterpreting the unraveling of this whole epidemic. Listen to this hypothetical phone call between "X" and "Y":

"Yo, what's crackin'?" says X . Y answers, "Ain't nothin', just chillin' wit' my wife tryin' to finish up dis here work."

Within this very short exchange of words, law enforcement agencies would have a field day drawing up arrest warrants. True, "What's crackin'?" is a term popularized by gangbangers, but it is also a greeting that is used by damn near every inner-city youth in existence. Sports figures, radio hosts, music recording artists... to them, "What's crackin'?" is the new hello. But, if a cop (or so-called expert) hears this exchange of words, "X" is immediately labeled a gang-member, and "Y" becomes a person of interest just because he used the word "work" in a sentence. For all we know, "X"· could have just gotten off work and called "Y" because he was bored out of his mind while "Y" and his wife were trying to have a nice night together. I understand the concept of "better safe than sorry"; however, the police change their communication codes numerous times a day-shouldn't they think that gangbangers do the same thing? Now, this is the real kicker: pay attention... the above scenario between "X" and "Y" happened! I'm "Y", and my best friend (who I'll continue referring to as "X") called me one day as he always did. The so-called experts had my phone tapped, and since "X" used some words that are a big part of urban culture, the so-called experts labeled him an underling of mine. Now, "X" is serving a fifty-year sentence all because he called to inquire about my well-being. The man never broke a sweat, let alone a damn law! He chose the path to the right, and I chose the left-yet; he is serving five decades because of his true friendship and because the so-called experts don't know how to decipher a wiretap.

Another thing the so-called experts misunderstand is a thing called "stackin'" (a way of communicating by use of the hands). Stackin' looks something like sign language. And every body talks with their hands nowadays.

The Italians have done it for decades but let a Black or Latino youth be seen waving to his girlfriend across the street, and the cops will think they just made the gang bust of the century.

A funny story about stackin': during the summer of 2003, personnel from inside the Trenton Police Department allegedly decided that they wanted to make a profit off of this sickness that is destroying our young people. Several members of the Anti-Crime Unit thought it would be of some pleasure to videotape dozens of young gang-bangers performing the art of stackin'. Many gang members recorded "B-Walkin'" (a dance performed by Blood members) or just trash-talking to anyone willing to listen. Months later, this recorded video was in almost every Mom & Pop store in the city of Trenton. Not only did the Police Department glamorize and popularize the art of stackin', but they fattened their pockets with proceeds from the videos!

Do you want to know why your loved one joined a gang? I don't know why-I don't really care! I know why he or she stayed, though. They stayed because there was nothing left for them to take home. Because of pop culture and urban culture, they are being characterized as gang members anyway because there are others like them that gravitate toward them and give them a sense of acceptance and belonging-others that give them strength in numbers. Because the so-called experts knowingly or unknowingly advertise attractive components of your loved one's addiction. The deck is stacked against them, and we need to thoroughly examine each card as we begin dealing our young ones a new deck. If not... the cancer shall remain irreversible.

* * * * *

Chapter 3
Short Story

The crime bill has criminalized affiliation. It is a declaration of war on black men. The section of the law on gangs and cocaine tells the tale.
- Mumja Abu-Jamal

Chapter 3:
Short Story

It's been three years since my last hit-since my last dose of gangbangin'. I used to wear my gang colors like a badge of honor. When I wore my badge, I didn't fear death, I didn't fear prison, I didn't fear the law... I didn't fear that none of my crew did either...

In the fall of 2004:

It was my set's year; that's what I thought. My team was called the Bounty Hunter Bloods, and we had the reputation of being the most notorious gang in the country, a notoriety we lived up to very well.

One night, the air was cool, and crisp-the urge to be out and about just couldn't be resisted. I got dressed- my normal dress: bulletproof vest, 9 mm on the hip, leather jacket; fresh (brand new) pair of Chuck Taylor Converse sneakers, and of course they were red... blood red.

I was in the mood to hit the local hole-in-the-wall, have a drink, and toss back a few with the crew, but before I could do that, I had to head across town and pick up a couple of my homies "goons" are what they were really called. In the hood, the term "goon" is used to describe a mindless lunatic- someone who's addicted to puttin' in work and doesn't care about anything. Anyway... about an hour prior, I got a call telling me that some of my adversaries were out of bounds. They had the nerve to be hanging in my bar! That's a rule everyone knew would bring death if it was broken. There's no stompin' in another set's hood- I don't care who you are.

My mind immediately transformed into killer mode. That's what a gangbanger considers "bein' on point". The adrenalin surged through my body as if raw caffeine or pure cocaine pumped through my veins instead of blood. Even if I wanted to-and I'm not saying that I did-there was no way I could thwart my thirst for blood that night. Knowing my enemy was nearby gave me a rush of energy, and it had to be released somehow. It was midnight, and all the fake killers were out-I say fake because a real killer walks the earth any time of day. The sky was painted black, dend the wind was blowing danger through the air. I'm numb, and so is my crew; we don't wanna hear anything about no laws or innocent bystanders on the street. Finding yourself in our way that night was nothing but a funeral waiting to happen.

"There they go!" someone shouted.

That's all it took for me to pull my G-ride to the side of the road. We got out of the car; my goon D-boy was strapped with an AK-47 Russian Assault Rifle while me and my lil' homie Hood stayed hidden in the darkness with two Mossberg-pump shotguns. That quick, we went from G-Mackin' (slang term for hanging out) to mission mode.

The door to the bar swung open, and I canvassed the area like my eyes were digital cameras. I spotted them, but before I could lay down my law, Hood let the Mossberg go (slang for started shooting). D-boy joined in with him and let the chopper rip.

"Yeah! What's poppin' now!?! Take that... take that!"

I never understood why D-boy would scream at a person while he was trying to make them gain some lead weight. They could never hear me because the Mossberg filled the room with blasts of loud thunder every half-second, and the chopper filled in the silent gaps resembling the sound of a lawn mower being started over and over. I felt like an NFL quarterback trying to make my receiver catch a pass.

The smoke cleared. The bar stools were empty. The place wasn't that full to begin with. There was so much shattered glass I almost mistook the shards for the bar's new carpeting. The clowns we were shooting at were either supernatural, or me and my homies had drunk too much because we didn't hit a goddam thing.

Later, we found ourselves lying back at the Honeycomb Hide-out. The Honeycomb was a house that I and my team bought so most of the crew could hang hats or just chill out. Mostly, we conducted business there, though. Once we arrived, Shamika was a nervous wreck. She was the chick we relied on to keep the Honeycomb intact. She cooked, cleaned, and did our laundry; basically, she did whatever I told her to.

We kept police scanners in all the bedrooms upstairs, with three homies listening and always learning. So, of course, when the shooting occurred in the bar across town, Shamika got the minute-by-minute from all the police chatter over their radios. She was the first one to contact me on my chirp-phone to tell me that the Jakes were heading to the bar.

We were all excited and heated at the same time-excited because we all made it out of the bar alive, heated because we shot off twenty rounds and didn't shoot anybody (we were literally upset about not killing anyone)! We quickly shed out of our murderous skins like anaconda snakes and went right back to G-Mackin. The first thing D-Boy did was roll up a blunt of sour-D, then he cranked the volume to the radio until the gangster sounds of The Game's first album shook the Honeycomb walls like a Cali quake.

We kept all our guns downstairs in the basement, and not just our guns, but our bullet-proof vests and our women; it was like a VIP room in the back of a strip club. There was nothing but weed smoke and butt-naked women loving the scene of some young, rich gangsters. I enjoyed their company all night until my phone rang again. It was my girl-Tee. She was screaming on the other end like a crazed woman. "Gullie, where you at!?!" she shouted. "What time are you coming home?" It never failed; Tee kept track of my whereabouts like a parole officer does a parolee. She wasn't a stupid woman; Tee was aware of the gang wars that broke out in the city. She knew about all the beef between sets, and even more, she knew if there was some gunplay going on somewhere, my team and I were right in the thick of it. After Tee nagged me for what seemed like hours to come home, she told me she had heard about the shooting and that she was worried about me.

"Aight," I said, "I'll be there in a minute."

Tired and drunk off my ass, I made my way to my G-ride with two armed guards accompanying me. A little while back, another one of my homies' named Denver Lane was gunned down, so my crew thought it best to keep me heavily guarded. I felt powerful, like I was President Obama, and my team was the Secret Service.

I made it home, opened the front door, and disarmed the ADT alarm system. I staggered into the bedroom and saw my newborn baby boy and Taliah (Tee) wide awake, waiting for me. I smiled, lay on the bed, and just like that, I switched from gangster to family man... what a night.

* * * * *

Chapter 4
Accountability

" Everything revolves around buying and selling, promoting, and advertising. This logic leads ultimately to the Gangsterization of culture, the collapse of moral fabric, and the shunning of personal responsibility in both vanilla suburbs and chocolate cities."

Dr. Cornel West

1994

Chapter 4:
Accountability

Accountability: accepting the idea of something able to be explained; accepting the idea of being called to answer for something; the idea of being explicable.

We must begin to ask ourselves (we, as in those individuals who perpetuate the underworld of gang violence)-are we holding ourselves accountable for the havoc that we continue to cause in our communities? This question may seem a bit shocking because this is the first junction of my book where I am talking directly to anyone and everyone who is addicted to the death style.

Taking on a sense of responsibility forces a person into a mindset of decision making. Now, the idea of accountability is not something that is easily taught or learned. To give you a small example-have you ever ridden the elevator with a large group of people? All of you pack yourselves in. The shy person cowers toward the back. The confident one wedges his way to where the control buttons are. The snooty person-even if there is room elsewhere will stand as close to the elevator doors as possible just to keep distance from the rest of the crowd. The garrulous one will start chatting up uninteresting conversations because people are forced to endure him for the next thirty seconds or so...And then it happens...somebody lays a fart! You hear it, you smell it, none of you are detectives, but it doesn't take one to figure out who did it. Yet, most people will deny something as natural as farting until their very last breath.

Suppose we can't accept responsibility for something as mundane and natural as flatulence. In that case, I think it's going to be a tall task asking people to willingly answer for the senseless atrocities that they may have committed in their communities. With this being the case, I'm not telling all of you gangbangers out there to go running into the nearest police station and tell them where you were last night (however noble that may be). I'm merely asking you to hold yourself accountable before you make the decision to "smoke" one of your enemies who, unbeknownst to you, was on his way to USC next week on a football scholarship. I'm asking you to hold yourself responsible for the young ones who run, skip, and play in the streets of our neighborhoods. They play games of Tag, Hide-n-Seek, and Cops and Robbers, yet none of the kids want the role of the cops because they see the gangbangers in the street and want to be just like them. If the kids want your 200.00-dollar sneakers, fine; let them have them. They want your shiny jewels, your fast cars, your bulletproof vests, and your semi-automatics. You keep all of that to yourself, except, of course, for that bullet that struck a little girl in her face, which you intended for someone else. Don't you think it would be much easier to prevent this sort of thing than it would be to try to explain why you let it happen in the first place?

Accountability falls upon all of us; at least it sure seems that way when a little boy gets run down by a drunk driver. The whole neighborhood lines up in the streets telling news reporters what they saw and how wonderful the kid's family is. But, when the cameras are gone, the people are back in the liquor stores. They return to the Lottery lines, trying to remember all their children's birthdays. Some are on the prowl again for the local dealer, and never once do they think to themselves that the money they drank away, gambled away, or shot in their veins could be used to uplift their community somehow. I know many of you remember the Black Wall Street Era. That's when the men of our impoverished neighborhoods began to take control of our economic situation. Everybody from street vendors to car-trunk salesmen to investment bankers began popping up throughout our streets. What slowed down Black Wall Street? It was the hate from white Tulsans that led to what many black historians describe as a "race war" and not a "race riot". White mobs of people looted and burned down Greenwood (Black Wall Street) strategically plotted and planned the demise of so many black Tulsans. The times became more desperate, which led to young men and women (boys and girls) literally waking up and thinking of creative ways to disrespect and or hurt one another. The heroin, the crack, the gun battles over turf, the degrading of our women, and the shaming of our men...the list is endless! But so is your potential and capability toward righteousness. You! Yes, you right there... you, the gangbanger!

That woman you love to disrespect is still a queen, no matter how small or large her kingdom may be. That man whom you take pleasure in degrading is still a keeper and a protector, no matter how great or little his family is. You may disagree, and you may get angry with me but know that I am only trying to prevent the graveyards and penitentiaries from having their fill because of nonsense.

I remember the summer of 2004; I decided to take a trip out to Detroit, Michigan. A few of my old running partners had some family out there, so we would usually try to visit at least twice a year. As I look back, I can see that each trip was a slap in my face as I noticed the scenery becoming stranger and stranger. I couldn't help but notice that on every block we rode down, there were, at a minimum, two or three dilapidated houses or businesses that obviously once thrived. I know for a fact they used to thrive because I frequented them. As we drove further along East Warren Street, it wasn't long before we spotted the local D-boy (dope dealer) driving in what most dope dealers refer to as "old school, " a car that is a classic, like a 55 Monte Carlo or a tricked out 67 Chevy. No horns blowing, just the raising of two fingers slightly spread apart like the peace sign. But, in The D (slang for Detroit), they call that Chuckin the Deuce. It was nothing but a sign of familiarity between gangbangers. Then, a chirp from my Nextel phone brings my conversation to an end.

"Yo, they just killed Taco!" echoed the voice on the other end. All I did was lean back in the seat, grab my bottle of Patron, which I kept in my lap for easy access, and lit my Dutch that was stuffed with Sour D. I was numb to the news of the death of my homie because that happened so frequently in my world. The neighborhood had gone into shambles; black men and women were getting murdered around me (by other black men and women); the only thing I could think to do was dump some 90-proof alcohol in my stomach and some marijuana in my lungs-no accountability whatsoever.

Being accountable meant I had to learn how to become a protector of my people. When he or she was down, I had to be willing to lift them. In the slums, we tend to slap a person's hand away when all they are doing is reaching for a way to get up. Our people have exhausted themselves. They have taken so much from others that they now have no choice but to start taking from themselves. The young twenty-year-old female college student starts selling what's between her legs, and the promising athlete is either buying the sex from her or helping her sell it. Sooner or later, they have nothing left of themselves, nothing in their homes. Even the newborn baby is gone because something in their addicted minds told them that it was okay to sell it for five thousand dollars.

My stepfather told me that it takes a village to raise a child. Hmph-if he was alive today, he would probably tell me to forget about that village and find myself a nation to help save our babies. The problem with that is... the nation is overrun with gangbangers. The upside to that is the gangbangers are highly influential. They just need to channel their influence elsewhere. Feed the young children who are hungry and stop slapping their hands away by splashing them with stray bullets. They are searching for nourishment, so give it to them! Not the nourishment filled with your bullet-proof vests and your gang wars. Give them that mental and spiritual nourishment that will stick around for a lifetime. You do that, and sooner or later, we can start referring to our communities as "neighborhoods" again instead of "hoods". This is true accountability. So hold yourselves accountable.

Chapter 5
Death Style

Did you know that if you put turtles in an aquarium and don't feed them...they will soon eat one another?

    - Known Study.

Chapter 5:
Death Style

Obvious thread throughout these pages is the term "Death Style". It is only fitting that we look at this word (death) for a moment. According to Merriam-Webster's Dictionary, death is the end of life, the cause of loss of life, the cause of ruin; the state of being dead; destruction; extinction.

When I use the term "Death Style", it is not to degrade an individual; rather, it is to tell the reality of the nature and culture of gang-bangin'. When the result of a circumstance is either death, prison, or becoming some corrupt cop's informant, there is no more befitting term to coin this way of life other than something synonymous with death.

Death, no matter how glorious a picture we paint, is going to be a common denominator in all our lives. It is the result of literally everything! You will become very acquainted with death, as will your children, your neighbors, your religious leaders, your soul mate, your idols, your first kiss, your last kiss- all of them... ALL OF US will meet death. The question is...how?

The best way for me to describe a gangbanger's concept of death is through vampirism. A vampire walks the earth already dead with a variety of supernatural abilities that make a vampire impervious to the fears and causes of death. Why would such a creature fear death when it is already dead? A vampire roams the night in thirst for blood- the one thing it cannot live without. This very much describes the actions of a gangbanger. These sorts of people stampede around (mostly at night) with their automatic weapons in search of loss of life. They are fearless, and they don't know why. They believe they can't be killed; even after one of their "homies" is shot dead, it doesn't convince the gangbanger that death is patiently or impatiently awaiting him/her. And I understand-remember I forged the path in which the gangbanger is traveling right now. I felt invincible! I carried weapons on which I placed more value than I did my children! I didn't know it at the time, but that's exactly what I did. At any moment, I could have been stripped of existence, and my children would have been left fatherless in a world where the value of life is ever waning. I lived as the gang members of today live without a moral compass. My subconscious mind told me that I was already dead, which made me unable to contemplate actual death. The gangbanger in me had to die so that the man in me could live. It's a hard lesson learning that life and death are one in the same. Gangbangers...do your best to kill the vampire in you!

I can remember lying in my cell one day listening to an A.M. broadcast of Pastor Tony Evans. He said something that day that washed away every bit of confusion I ever had about why some of my people were in such a dead state. He said something along the lines that our children are running rampant or astray because the "bull elephant" is no longer keeping order in the household. He further explained how a group of people conducted an experiment on a herd of African Elephants. The Bull Elephant was removed from the rest of the herd. As a result, the younger calves seemed to shed the cloak that held back their inhibitions. The calves literally ran wild and ventured off into terrains in which they had never gone. Without guidance, they broke the laws of their natural habitat. However, once the Bull Elephant was returned, the younger calves noticeably flapped their ears and showed other signs of happiness.

The Bull Elephant is missing in many homes today. As a result, the children are transgressing against the laws of society. Please do not mistake these words for a guess or mere opinion. I, too, was a young calf missing the bull. This caused me to develop deep feelings of resentment, anger, frustration...abandonment. I was hurt, Thus the saying "Hurt people... will hurt people". So, how do we reunite the bull with the calf? How do we change the cycle of the "Death Style"?

Well, for one thing, we must start rehabilitating people. I said, rehabilitating people-not just the drug dealers or the gangbangers, but everybody. The ones in prison need programs (real programs) that will force them to kill the vampires within themselves. The ones who have escaped the law need to be taught the importance of recapturing the title of the bull. The children must be dealt with patiently as they undergo self-imposed rehabilitation that makes them realize they no longer must survive without the bull. The mother, one who proves herself to be stronger and stronger with each passing day, needs to understand that, though she is very capable of maintaining her household by herself, she doesn't have to. As for the ones outside of the family, the neighbors, the lawmakers, the teachers, the role models, do your part without having to be asked. It is said that experience is the best teacher, and that may be true, but so is good character. Good character is supported by ideas such as patience, understanding, leniency, compassion, etc. These are characteristics that the gangbanger possesses but, for some reason, chooses to ignore. So, we CAN'T ignore them. Compassion needs to be shown on every level when dealing with the Death Style-from-the victim, the criminal, the lawyer, the judge, to the lawmaker. If not, then there is no way for rehabilitation to find its way inside the malicious cycle of crime and punishment.

The "Death Style" has claimed the lives of well over eighty of my old friends. Eighty is an insignificant number in the grand scheme of things, but just imagine if you came to know and love eighty different people and then had to watch each of them die. I'm talking about people of all ages from the old lady who reminds you of your grandmother to the young preteen strutting around his hood with an assault rifle. People deal with sorrow differently, but most can't handle the loss of one person, let alone eighty! And that's what the "Death Style" brings. It magnifies the concept of ill will. It promotes and glorifies all things wicked and impure, and it does this under the guise of becoming part of a brotherhood or protecting one's turf.

Transformation is imperative when we speak of ridding ourselves of the "Death Style". But the only transformations that are visible to me are the physical ones. Our children grow wider and taller, but their minds remain as narrow as ever. I know it is a tall task to overcome with things like TV and the internet counterbalancing our constructive efforts. But, the TV, the internet, video games, cinema...these things are like food to the average young person, and any nutritionist will tell you that there is poison in every food we can eat. The good news? There is also benefit in these things as well. It is going to be necessary to use these tools along with many others to save the people we love...in order to save ourselves from the "Death Style".

Chapter 6
Gang-Bangin' Mothers

"No man, for any considerable period, can wear one face to himself, and another to the multitude, without finally getting bewildered as to which may be true."

    -Nathaniel Hawthorne
    1850

The statistics in this chapter concerning the cost to house, clothe, and feed an inmate have astronomically changed. Several of the prisons listed in this chapter have since been closed. #EndMassIncarceration.

Chapter 6:
Gang-Bangin' Mothers

Does a mother with an addiction love her child? Yes, of course, she does. However, when the seizing power of her addiction is at its strongest, the very nature of the situation calls for the child to be neglected. The same can be said of a gang-bangin' mother.

Once a woman becomes aligned with a gang, she is subjected to certain behaviors, as is anybody else. The lifestyle does not discriminate; her existing creed becomes meaningless, as does her ethnicity and her color. Once she takes on the complexion of a gang, it begins to eat her alive from the inside out.

Her priorities change. The grandparents now don the title of parents. For most of these young women, there was a father figure, but he no longer an interest in her upbringing. The father of her child (or children) is off impregnating another young woman, dampening her dreams, and poisoning her potential. The idea of being abandoned engulfs the woman from every angle. From her father to the young man who helped her spawn a child, the role of masculinity in her life begins to wane seriously. What does this bring about? The nothingness of a void? Promiscuity in search of promise? Derelict dating? In my experience, I've found that all these things occur, and the woman, often, is oblivious to the transformation.

She turns to the guy who always smiles at her when she walks to the corner store in search of diapers for her baby. She seeks the man who paid for her bottle of champagne one night, not knowing that the man believes he's actually paid for something else. What else doesn't she know? She doesn't know that she fits the profile of the type of promising young lady that gang members are looking for.

She meets a gangbanger; he secures her and represents strength. She begins to act like him, walk like him, talk like him. Her favorite food is the same as his. She sleeps when he sleeps and wakes when he wakes. Her identity, her being is sneakily transformed. She's no longer herself because if her new homies don't like something, neither does she. Dependency develops. Her ability to think individually is weakened, not removed, and she now fits the definition of a captive. Think about it: what is the sole purpose of torture? To break a person's will, to get them thinking as you want them to think so they can do as you wish for them to do. It's astounding, really...most gangbangin' mothers are torture victims, yet they feel as if the world is theirs. Notice, throughout her transformation, never once was there a mention of her children at home.

Now, the child is subject to be reared without its father or mother. The cycle sneaks its way into every generation. Many of the parents in the gang-bangin' population today were either 'high rollers' or dope addicts in the early eighties. And their parents were the Rolling Stones of their day-the generational curse continues.

So, do we lock the women up like we've done the men? Stack them and cage them, leaving them to wallow in their own disease and addiction? Is prison the foreseen answer here, too? To deliver diseased men and women into the hands of further diseased men and women?

Did you know that in the state of New Jersey, it costs $54,233 to house a female inmate? Or that the New Jersey Department of Correction's total budget tops one billion dollars? It literally costs more money to send a person to prison than it does to send them to college! Significantly more! Tuition at one of New Jersey's finest institutions, Princeton, is $37,000. Compare this figure to the cost of the incarcerated:

Taxpayers Dollars

Correctional Facility	Annual Cost
New Jersey State Prison	$44,734
Vroom Central Reception and Assignment Facility	$45,309
East Jersey State Prison	$44,817
South Woods	$34,185
Bayside	$28,698
Southern State	$29,178
Mid State	$41,241
Edna Mahan Facility for Women	**$54,233**
Northern State	$32,799
Adult Diagnostic and Treatment Center	$54,427
Wagner Youth Correction Center	$39,995
Mountainview Youth Facility	$36,931

*Figures projected for fiscal year (2010). Statistics: NJ Dept. of Corrections; NJ Dept. of Treasury. Source: Trentonian.

* * * * *

The addition to gang-bangin' attacks the female in the same manner as it does the male. Putting in work gives the female the same adrenalin rush. Remember, she begins to think, act, speak, walk, and desire in the same fashion as her new father figure. The innate sense of care that existed within the woman is misplaced. The fact she has given birth or is capable of such doesn't ring loudly in her ear·s anymore. Now, it's the echo of an AK-47 or some other similar instrument of death. This sort of woman needs to be rescued. How can she nurture the children of the future when she has been trained to forget the conditions of Her nurturing?

* * * * *

Chapter 7
The Crown that Doesn't Exist

"Three may keep a secret if two of them are dead."
    Benjamin Franklin- 1728

Chapter 7:
The Crown that Doesn't Exist

Ancient civilizations teach us through pictorials and hieroglyphics about those among them in authority. We see that the kings wore the finest crowns, and the queens were adorned with the rarest of draping jewels. A crown, according to Merriam-Webster's Dictionary, is a mark of victory or honor, The title of a champion in some sort of sport.

I've already introduced you to one of the most brutal sports on the planet. There is no Super Bowl in this sport, no divisional playoffs, and no shiny trophy waiting for you at the end. All you have is the coach, which is the gang leader, your teammates, who are nothing but your gang-bangin' friends (I use the term loosely), and you have the opposing team that sometimes doesn't even play by the same set of rules as you. Then you have the practice field and the game field...the streets.

War occurs at the start of game time. The idea in any sporting contest is to outdo your opponent in every physical and mental way imaginable. If your opponent is fast, you drill to increase your speed. If he or she is strong, you train to magnify your strength. If one is more physical than you, you train to outthink them; if they are smarter, you attempt to overwhelm them with brute force. In the realm of sport and play, everything literally everything- revolves around the concept of conquering and defeating. One team must and will mow down the other to obtain the title of being the very best. The only problem is that in football or baseball, there is a crown awaiting the victor at the end of the journey; in gang-bangin', there is nothing at the end of the journey...except the end of the journey. The crown of prestige and power doesn't exist in this sport. Very few even live long enough to make it through the first "away game".

It doesn't matter if it is two gang sets beefin' over drug turf, vying for women, acquiring the most expensive and nonsensical things or four cars or boats, just as many homes, designer clothes, flashy jewelry. The gangbanger risks his or her life for these things because the gangbanger feels the appearance of such possessions provides power. There is absolutely nothing wrong with wanting to have such things. The wrong is committed due to the way one goes about obtaining one's wealth.

When I was in the game, I was addicted to the chase. I found myself constantly in beast mode. If I saw something that I wanted, rest assured that

I was going to get it. Anyone in my way was interfering with the shine of my crown-and that is the quickest way to bring out the beast in any member of the game. I was a tyrannical king wearing a sought-after crown. The gangbangers in my set wanted my crown, my enemies wanted it, hell, even the police wanted it. Do you know how incredibly stupid I felt when I discovered that the crown never existed? At least, not the crown I was searching for.

People wonder why a gangbanger falls into the trap of doing the same things over and over. "He disrespected me, so I gotta kill him!" "They gotta die because they gettin' money in my hood!" "Don't nothin' happen in these streets without my say-so!" These are some of the things that we say trying to win a prize that is a figment of the imagination. There is no on top, no king of the hill; there is only the climb of reaching the top of the hill and the fall, which is usually rapid. Most of the time, before you get there, someone is already plotting to take your life so they can get there first. And somebody is planning to take that person's life, and the next person's, and the next! I say again, the crown does not exist! All that awaits the gangbanger is a prison... or the morgue. Now, the morgue awaits us all. But the gangbanger arrives sooner than most.

That hunger, that feel of the chase, it's not a physical possession; I believe it's much more profound than that. The gangbanger is missing something or someone, so he or she creates a trophy that is impossible to obtain. That's what happens when one tries to fill a void; they try to fill it with something intangible. They fill that void with delusions, and they are incapable of realizing what it is they are really missing...what it is they are really searching for. Ask yourself:

1. What's your name? Where are you from? And what gang do you claim?

2. When did you get initiated into the gang?

3. Tell us about some of your experiences as a gang member. What was it like?

4. Tell us about your family. Your mother. Your father. Do you have any sisters or brothers?

5. What was it like growing up with your family?

6. What was school like when you were growing up?

7. Prior to becoming a gang member, did you have any aspirations? What did you want to be when you grew up?

8. At what point in your life did you decide that you were going to participate in what is known as the "Under World"?

9. Have you ever been incarcerated?

10. If so, did you ever have an encounter with God?

11. What led you to join a gang?

12. When you joined the gang, did you realize that you were signing away the rest of your life?

13. What type of psychological effects do you believe being in a gang has had on you?

14. Living in such a reality, have you ever contemplated your death?

15. Have you ever thought about the reasons why you would die?

16. Having thought about such an end, have you ever contemplated a course of action that would change your fate?

17. If you have accepted your end, do you believe that the next generation (young people) should submit themselves to the philosophy and principles that govern the underworld?

18. Can you think of a solution that will end this epidemic I like to call the "Death Style"?

19. Do you believe in a standard of living that encompasses morals and ethics? If so, where do you adopt your standard from?

20. Is there a message you would like to convey to the next generation?

Contract

I______________________, promise to end the death style of gang-banging today! I am taking full responsibility for the rebuilding of the neighborhood I once tore down. The deadly cycle of violence will stop with me. I will break the generational curse that has plagued my family for years. Today, I take a stand, standing for those who are dead and gone, those who died while struggling for change. I will be a productive member of my family and society.

Name (print)

Name (sign)

Date

Chapter 8
Shell Shock

" It is highly probable that the majority of the kids growing up in these war-torn communities across the country may have PTSD and or what is known as complex stress."

Dr. Monroe, Ph.D.

Chapter 8:
Shell Shock

Many people, young people particularly, do not know that they suffer from this mental illness - PTSD, also known as shell shock. Anyone who has undergone an attack of warfare fits this category. The experts in the medical field say that PTSD or shell shock is the result of fatigue due to exposure to combat. They also say that PTSD can easily be triggered by TBI (Traumatic Brain Injury). Webster's II New College Dictionary defines shell shock as any of various, usually acute, often hysterical, neuroses originating in trauma suffered under fire in modern warfare: combat fatigue. These are the reasons why a CT scan is so important - a high degree of accuracy is needed to properly locate any type of cerebral disorder.

A constant theme I've tried to convey is that most of our young men and women are at war in their communities throughout the slums of America. They are at war over money, power, and respect. They even go to battle over the city blocks which they don't even own. Their lives are transformed into actual war zones! After so many years of suffering and witnessing the loss of life, after so much violence and death, the human brain begins to tell its host that it can only take so much before it is forced to weaken the nervous system.

Anyone with good enough hearing will jump or shudder at the sound of a slamming door. But, for the people I'm talking about, for those who have been through what I've been through, the sound of a slamming door is not just something you flinch at. To me, it's a reminder of somebody kicking the door in so they can put two in my head while I'm sleeping! It's a shock mechanism that awakens a childhood monster I worked so hard to put to sleep. If a door slams or if a car backfires, sweat will instantly drench my face and armpits. You may say this can be true for anyone, and you would be correct in saying so. However, it's not the startling sound that gives people like me fear; it's what the sound has the potential to awaken. It's the reminder of what I used to be that chills my entire spine.

People like me, plus a crowded mall, equals paranoia. An innocent shoulder bump at a dance club or slight eye contact with a friend or foe will effectuate a response of defense. If I'm driving, my eyes are fixated on the rear-view mirror; it's not because I'm being cautious of the drivers behind me; rather, it's due to my thinking that someone, somewhere, is out to get me. I can't count how many drivers on the road I've frightened...all because I thought they were driving behind me too long.

Does that sound like the behavior of a normal person? To me, it sounds like a soldier who was shot down out of his jet plane and forced to land in enemy territory-in other words...a war zone.

The inner cities of Philadelphia, PA-war zone! Little Rock, Ark-war zone! South and West sides of Chicago-war zone! Gary, Ind...9th Ward of New Orleans...Watts, CA... war zone! War zone! War zone! The list goes on. These are just some of the bloodiest streets in the United States.

Imagine a child being reared in a place where a gun battle is as common as a kid with a skateboard. The echoing thunderous sound of bullets being fired, police sirens, smoke from burning buildings...all these things are indicative of what a soldier experiences in combat.

So many, many, many gangbangers want to get out of their respective war zones. But every time they find themselves doing right, every time they take a small step in a big direction, the sound of the slamming door wakes up the paranoid soldier inside of them.

I met the honorable Dr. Cornell West once during an open forum inside New Jersey State Prison. An inmate asked Dr. West, "How come every time I try to do something good for myself or someone else, I can't?" Dr. West's response didn't knock me out of my seat physically, but it sure felt like it. He looked the inmate directly in his eyes and told him, "You couldn't do good because you didn't have a moral compass. You were morally constipated which meant that you knew what doing right was all about, but just couldn't get it out." That's a saying that'll stick with you, and it's a saying our young brothers and sisters stuck in the war zone need to hear.

Symptoms to look for concerning PTSD:

* Anxiety or nervousness

* Depression or deep sadness

* Flashbacks and nightmares

* Trouble sleeping

* Memory suppression

* Dependency upon controlled substances (alcohol or drugs) to gain calmness

The term "Shell shock" became famous when this country's veterans began returning home from World War II; it was also referred to as "Battle Fatigue". Eventually, those terms graduated to PTSD, especially during the Vietnam War. It took years, almost decades, before the medical world would recognize PTSD as an illness that required serious treatment. Only recently have they discovered that an individual suffering from PTSD experiences what is known as "blackout periods." In other words, these people commit acts of violence without any knowledge of doing so!

This is one of the driving forces that propels my passion towards helping my brothers and sisters. All things gloomy can't remain in the dark; it is the natural order of things. It is my job, and the job of others like me, to shed light upon this dreary topic. The so-called cure of "lock'em up and throw away the key" is a complete failure. There shall come a time when this way of thinking shall be avoided altogether. The powers that be will have to realize that it causes more damage and costs more money to "house'em" instead of "treat'em".

It was all good when the gangs were solely infesting the inner cities but look at the suburbs now. It's not just a Black and Latino thing anymore, and white suburbia is slowly transforming into the new war zone. It's young people going to prison, and anytime a nation has more of its young people going to prison or the graveyard instead of college, there must be a huge problem at hand that many seem to overlook or simply refuse to recognize.

Here's a shocking realization for you... Shell shock is real.

* * * * *

Chapter 9
The Pledge

The one who knows much...has a lot to lose.
  -Dewan Dennis

Chapter 9:
The Pledge

My mother, and I'm sure many other mothers, used to say that money doesn't grow on trees. With the blows this nation's economy has taken lately, I'm certain that the inner-city urban communities are in dire need of cash flow. Let's face it: poverty is the main ingredient to the breeding grounds of violence.

I shouldn't have to recap the drawn-out list of ailments plaguing the youths of this nation. A blind person can see that drug and alcohol abuse are too rampant nowadays. It doesn't take a Ph.D. in psychology to understand that many young people today have serious mental defects. We know what's wrong; the world knows, but amid all this knowing, no one seems to know what to do.

My leisure reading time used to be spent reading books that outlined in detail all the ailments in the slums of America. Each book had a magnetic lock on my brain...until I reached the end of each book. Why? Not one of these books purported any feasible solutions if they even offered a solution at all. I've seen it! The death, the loss of life, the two-week-old baby being ripped from the clutches of its mother because its mother's addiction to crack was stronger than her will to do good.

I've witnessed blood (innocent and guilty) stain the pavement because of meaningless yet crucial conflicts. The number of so-called friends I've lost (wiped from this earth) is well into the hundreds. The number is just as great for all those I used to run with whose new turf is the state penitentiary.

After seeing the destruction, from both receiving and causing it, after hearing the same people constantly complain about what needs to be done while they show no action, I've decided to propose a pledge to any and every one who can and will be affected by the "Death Style".

If you are serious about eradicating the disease of gang-bangin', if you have experienced love and loss, if you have ever been wronged, if you have ever wronged somebody...then this pledge is for you. Your money is needed- you spend wastefully daily; don't you think it's time you spend in the way of something that shall protect the lives of your young ones? Your time is needed; no one knows when their time shall run out, so spend it bettering yourself and those around you. Your patience and perseverance are needed, the mighty Creator took His time creating the world when he could have easily done so in a single day.

If you don't have money, dedicate your time. If you don't have time, remain patient when dealing with your struggles. The time and the means shall present themselves when you are ready to receive them. And I'm not talking about donating cash and time to charities; though charities are fine, they are obviously not enough. I'm talking about getting up, getting involved, and intervening.

And to all the people who have risen from the ashes and made it to stardom, to all the Beyoncé out there, the Lil' Waynes, the T.I.s, the Jay-Z's...Rick Ross, Alicia Keys, 50 Cent, Russel Simmons, Chris Brown, Rhianna, Kobe Bryant, Lebron James, Dwayne Wade, Snoop Dog, Ice Cube... All of you hip-hop stars, music artists, pro athletes, business execs... THESE ARE YOUR COMMUNITIES TOO!

Can we, celebrity or not, honestly sit back while the slums and ghettos are being plagued with problem after problem? While the same problems are spilling over into middle-class suburbia? Problems that are neutralizing our future children before our very eyes. The pledge is for everyone!

There may not be many non-profit organizations that focus solely on curbing gang violence, so this, in essence, is the perfect time to start or support one! Cease Fire and the Interrupters, both out of Chicago, are certainly in dire need of volunteers and or funds. Mothers Against Violence out of Philadelphia, Street Corner Resources out of New York...I'm sure they are going in the right direction. But even heading in the right direction one can become lost. To make our attempts successful, we need successful venues, treatment facilities, prevention centers, and effective halfway houses focusing strictly on gangbangers, therapists, psychologists, and doctors to run cat scans searching for any brain injuries that can trigger PTSD and illnesses of the like. Again, these sorts of ailments can only be properly discovered through a CT scan. PTSD can literally be the reason why so many of our youths today are so violent.

These things take serious effort, money, resolve, and painstaking durability. Remove the fear that you have of the monster (the gangbanger) so you can effectively deal with the monster. This generation IS GOING TO DIE DUE TO LACK OF KNOWLEDGE!

So... those who don't wish to die, those who wish to eradicate the Death Style, those who want a better life for their children...I implore you...take the pledge.

I____ promise to take a stand to help any and everyone (within my means) that suffers. from the crippling disease of "gang-bangin'". I pledge to donate my time, my expertise, my knowledge...I pledge to donate $1,000, $5,000, $10,000, or any amount greater or less than that to assist in the plight against gang violence. From this day forward, I am the keeper of my brother, my sister, and the children of my brother and my sister... THE PLEDGE!

"People don't really care what you know... unless they know that you care...".
..

      Unknown author

Chapter 10
The Cure

"The only reason I joined a gang was because I wanted to protect my little brother after he joined. We had just lost our mother...we were hurting.
    -Charles Johnson
    Former Blood Member

Chapter 10:
The Cure

The harsh reality is someone somewhere will be against this idea of treating, educating, and truly rehabilitating the so called domestic terrorist-the gangbanger. As I mentioned earlier, if we don't fight to cure the problems that affect all our communities, then it is as if we are choosing a dangerous situation for ourselves and our children. Why wait for the rebellious ten-year-old, whom everyone has labeled a problem child, to become fed up with concepts that he or she doesn't understand? Soon, the child becomes fifteen years of age, and you are no longer calling him or her a problem child, now they are the monsters that you read about in the papers and see on the news.

That little boy you refused to treat carjacks one day while you are out for a drive. Or maybe it's grocery shopping time, and he holds you and everybody else in the store at gunpoint; you put up a fight, there's a struggle, and the gun goes off, killing you or hurting or killing someone else there. You want to protect your possessions and your loved ones; I get it, I do, but this is the dangerous way of protecting what's yours. Don't think for a second that this fifteen-year-old kid, turned monster, is not going to shoot you. He's going to shoot you and everybody else who gets in his way.

Is this behavior, okay? Absolutely not! What has influenced this child to make him or her think that such a course of action is okay? Society's normal response is to have the child locked away, which will allow our criminal justice system the opportunity to ruin the child even further. The child goes into the system as a misguided and hardnosed teen, then comes out seasoned and more hardened as an adult whose mind is stuck in a time capsule. It's very possible that the next time the child sees the light of day, he'll be fifty years of age; yes, he will be half of a hundred! So, let's rewind this scene a bit. Let's go back to when this child was showing signs of rebellion - back to when he was ten, and this is when our intervention needs to come, right now! We need to ask the questions that no one dares to ask. Who is raising this child? What is this child's mental health history? What is the mental health history of the parents? Does this child take the bus to school, or does he walk because he's afraid of other children who are worse than him? Does this child walk to school, or is he being chased?

In any other scenario, the problem is diagnosed and then treated. So why not here, too? I can only speculate that this inner-city child is not worth your time and money because you desire a better way for all the privileged children of suburbia. If that's true, then we can no longer say the children are our future, we can only say some of them are.

I asked you about the ten-year old's behavior, now I'll ask about yours. Is this behavior, okay? Is it a good idea to beat'em instead of treat'em? We focus on our kid's behavior, when most of the time, we need to focus on our own.

If we sit back, if we feign contentment, then the result is more than likely what you see now-gang violence. I've said it before, and I'll say it again: gang violence has plagued this nation since the 1970's. If this epidemic were to affect middle-class suburbia and upper-class suburbia as it does the inner-city youths, this nation would undoubtedly be declared a state of emergency.

Forty-two years is a long time, but that's exactly how long we have been killing ourselves! There is no blame to be made except upon us. WE DID IT! That's why it's going to take the US to come up out of it.

Look around you; the liquor shop and the pawn shop are dime-a-dozen. Where's the fruit stand? The corner store and the bodega are just as plentiful in the urban community. Where are all the good grocery stores? I'll tell you, a good driving distance away from our community, that's where. It has been this way for as long as I can remember, and this is not a thing of racism or hatred. I'm just trying to awaken people to something I believe many of them would love to be a part of. Some of us see the wrong but have no idea of how to deal with it. It's like what Dr. Cornell West said, "People want to do the right thing but just can't because they are morally constipated."

I believe people want to do the right thing. I believe that YOU believe you want to do the right thing. But tell me, what is the right thing? If I believe and you believe, then what exactly do WE believe? What is the common creed between us? I don't expect you to have an answer for that question because I didn't have an answer... until a program entitled C.R.E.E.D. was brought to my attention.

What is C.R.E.E.D.?

Conflict Resolution through Education and Empowered Decisions

The title alone strikes hope within the hearts of those who hear it. C.R.E.E.D is that sort of program that every Boys' & Girls' club should implement everywhere. Every halfway house, every early release program, every juvenile detention center, every college or university... take your blinders off and pay strict attention to the following words. Because I am about to give you a cure to a sickness you didn't even know existed-a cure to the sickness of the deathstyle. A cure to gangbangin', not just a fix, like a prison or the grave, but an outright cure.

WHAT'S NEEDED?

Mental Health: C.R.E.E.D requires a Doctor of Clinical Psychology.

Reformed Gang Members: It's no longer the idea 'Of it takes a criminal to catch a criminal, rather, it takes a reformed criminal to reform a criminal. Former gang-bangers can easily relate to the participants of C.R.E.E.D...

Neuropsychologist/Neurologist/Sociologist: The participant's behavior must be monitored. Before the program and upon completion of the program, each participant must be given a CT scan. This helps to determine, if any, what brain disorders must be treated (PTSD or any other brain defects).

As stated earlier, if it is proven that those who have committed their lives to the deathstyle of gangbangin' suffer from the same symptoms that our soldiers in war suffer from (PTSD), then the gangbanger must be treated accordingly-especially if we are to say that PTSD is a mentally debilitating disease. Getting back to the explanation of C.R.E.E.D., please help me in helping a generation of future innovators. The C.R.E.E.D. Program can accomplish the following:

* Effective rehabilitation in the lives of men and women who have been deemed social deviants.

* Deterrent from engaging in negative behavior, such as, but not limited to, drugs and or gang activity.

* Assisting in creating an environment that will cultivate positive thinking and communication within society.

* Assisting in the participant's transition from reckless adolescents to responsibly thinking men and women.

THE CURRICULUM:

The curriculum consists of three lesson plans. Each lesson plan requires a minimum of four (4) weeks to complete. Three months is the projected duration for the entire program; however, time may vary.

LESSON PLAN 1 (week 1) - Moral Value Curriculum:

The thirty (30) participants, upon entry, will be split into two (2) groups - group 1 consisting of Blood gang members and group 2 consisting of Crip gang members (it does not matter if a participant is a member of another gang not mentioned). Each group will then select a representative to articulate their thoughts and ideas. A secretary will also be selected to take notes and act on behalf of the representative in his absence. Once these selections have taken place, a collective cross-reference begins. Group 1 writes down six (6) things they do not agree with about Group 2''s moral values, and Group 2 must do the same about Group 1. Every disagreement must have a detailed explanation, and it must be articulated by the selected representative. Then comes a moderated discussion of the details.

LESSON PLAN 1 (week 2) - The Rebuttal:

The representatives will have a second opportunity to express their group's particular dislikes about the other group's moral values. Each representative shall then provide a logical rebuttal.

LESSON PLAN 1 (week 3) - The Resolution:

Both groups will be required to prepare sensible resolutions for the dislikes that have been charged against them. The week shall be spent in preparation.

LESSON PLAN 1 (week 4) - Accord of Moral Values

The representatives of each group shall be awarded the opportunity to present their resolutions for the purpose of strengthening their moral values.
Abandonment Curriculum

LESSON PLAN 2 (week 5):

A compilation of questions will be presented for the purpose of establishing a level of trust and comfort between the two groups. Also, each participant will be required to stand for 2 to 3 minutes and speak about their childhood and upbringing.

LESSON PLAN 2 (week 6):

The members of Group 1 will be asked to identify three (3) distinct occurrences or factors that may have had a negative impact on their childhood or upbringing. Each point shall be equipped with an explanation to be articulated by the group representative. The task of this week is only for Group 1.

LESSON PLAN 2 (week 7):

Group 2 will be required to present three (3) ideas that they believe will allow Group 1 to embrace them as friends so that they may extract the necessary wisdom from each other's life experiences. The task of this week is only for Group 2.

LESSON PLAN 2 (week 8):

This is the time for reflection so the participants of each group may be able to recognize the manifestation of trust they are beginning to develop.

Community Solidarity Curriculum

LESSON PLAN 3 (week 9):

The course instructors shall orchestrate a presentation that will focus on the similarities between Group 1 and Group 2. This is a time when nothing will be asked of the participants except that they sit back and absorb the life lessons being presented by former gang members.

LESSON PLAN 3 week 10):

The course instructors shall establish the importance of unifying oneself with the moral values of the participant's families and communities. The change in moral value shall be identified within each participant.

LESSON PLAN 3 (week 11):

The course instructors shall establish the importance of a code of ethics. Each participant of each group will be shown how to apply and accept the code of ethics so that they may be able to function morally responsibly as individuals, as well as within a community.

LESSON PLAN 3 (week 12):

The course instructors shall provide all participants with a questionnaire designed to identify and establish the importance of effective change, effective change within the minds of today's youth, and tomorrow's community. The participants shall be encouraged to communicate a positive message to their perspective communities through all available means. One avenue of communication shall be by way of a letter writing campaign. The participants shall be encouraged to write letters to schools, places of worship, community outreach centers, county jails, prisons, and other facilities with access to vulnerable, at-risk youths who may benefit from the lessons of C.R.E.E.D.

The C.R.E.E.D program has been tried and tested on a smaller level. The results? 75% of the participants no longer indulge in negative behavior. The trial run was facilitated by a Doctor of Psychology, and most of the participants were members of various gangs. C.R.E.E.D., if properly implemented and magnified, can and will change lives. How do I know? Because I, Dewan "Gully Boy" Dennis, was a participant who successfully graduated!

The cure is in your hands now. What are you going to do with it? Are you going to wait until you are a victim of a drive-by shooting gone wrong? Are you going to let another innocent young girl be the recipient of a stray bullet? Let's face it...the world is sick, but I have the perfect medicine. Are we going to wait until more people get sick, or are we going to be preemptive with the cure? What do I think? I think we can change the world together...one patient at a time.

The following individual completed the CREED curriculum and would like to give a brief testimony about what he experienced during his time in the program.

Charles Johnson

Hello, my name is Charles Johnson, and I am 40 years old. I was born in Newark, New Jersey... "Brick City." I am currently incarcerated at New Jersey State Prison on a life sentence.

My story is like most kids growing up in Newark, New Jersey. I was raised in a single-parent household. My mother did her best to raise my siblings and me. When I was twelve, she passed away from natural causes. However, in my mind, nothing was natural about that. To lose a mother is the worst feeling in the world, let alone at the tender age of twelve. Not too long after, I dropped out of School and quit playing basketball. I was hurting and angry at the same time. With no one to turn to, someone to provide me with some sort of direction, I went to the Bloods Street gang. The reason I joined the gang wasn't because of the false sense of bother hood. I joined because my little brother had made the commitment to align himself with the blood after our mother died. So, I made a commitment that required me to be down for the set, no matter what, just to protect my little brother. It wasn't until I came to New Jersey State Prison that I began to change my life.

I give all honor to God because it was him who saved me from myself and from going straight to hell.

After meeting Dewan here at the Prison and hearing about his spiritual transformation, I quickly signed up for the C.R.E.E.D. program. My first session lasted about two hours. I was skeptical because the room was filled with active gangbangers, crips, and blood. At the time, blood and crips were at war, and many of the crips were not in the population because the blood had the numbers in the general population. As soon as the room filled with gangsters, crips, blood, and a few Latin kings, I quickly took notice of how Dewan gracefully walked around the room as if he was a professor at a university teaching class.

Dewan was an excellent teacher, and his material for the curriculum was profound. His passion for change was obvious, and his love for the people, all people (crip or blood), was noticeable. Within no time, Dewan became my mentor and spiritual leader. I've witnessed the C.R.E.E.D. program change so many people's lives; just to think about it brings me to tears. Today, I now mentor other active gang members using some of the knowledge I learned in the C.R.E.E.D. program.

My message to the youth: Please do not live your life so fast that you end up in the grave or in someone's prison, serving a life sentence. **WAKE UP BEFORE IT'S TO LATE!**

Community Development

1. **Community facelift:** To get all abandoned buildings and create a fund for those in the community to be able to purchase and build community centers upon the property. To repair pavements and sidewalks, plant trees, increase lighting, and clean up vacant lots- all with community involvement and financial assistance from government grants.

2. **Education**: To implement accelerated learning programs; teach STEM, some sort of trade, and some classes in finance, as well as money marketing. To upgrade technology in all Schools which are in the urban community. This includes fixing and bringing up to date all classrooms, teaching business and entrepreneurial classes.

3. **Health and welfare**: Construction of new clinics, health care, and dental clinics. Complete eye exams. And the testing of every child from grades K-8 for dyslexia, PTSD, and or complex stress. The establishment of effective daycare centers. Eliminate welfare and provide job training with full employment, which will be incentive-based for corporations that hire those in need of employment. Provide welfare assistance for older people.

4. **Law Enforcement**: To work with grass root organizations from within the community to deal with the mentally ill. The creation of a database that tracks citizen complaints concerning abusive Police Officers. The creation of a "buddy patrol" whereby members of youth organizations are paired up with Police, trained and educated, being able to walk the community. This will allow the Police to get a better perspective of the community they serve. Those who Police the community must live there. This will afford the Officer the ability to get an understanding of how to Police effectively those black and brown brothers and sisters within that community. All Police Supervisors must live within that community for at least five years.

5. Economic Development: Corporations, such as but not limited to Wal-Mart, McDonalds, and Pepsi, create an Urban Renewal Fund for the communities that they are geographically close to. It is these major corporations that are marketing their products/ foods to the black and brown communities, sucking the money out of the ghetto in which these corporations are strategically built by or in. Loans must be given to all black-owned businesses at a 3% annual interest, and they must be security-free; seventy-five percent of the people employed by the business in that community must be residents thereof. The creation of baby bonds to help level the financial playing field for all black babies born in the United States of America.

6. Housing.: The U.S. Housing and Urban Development regional administrator is to cite the owners of any "Project Housing" and or apartment complex for any gross violations of their contract with HUD and create a program that allows those Citizens within that community to purchase all vacant property at a low cost.

7. Government Accountability: The holding of local advisory councils. The establishment of a community-wide Governing council that represents all groups and grass-root organizations in the community. And the holding of monthly accountability sessions that provide status reports to the citizens from within the community.

The Cure.

Acknowledgements

I first give glory and honor to God for saving me and changing my life.

And to my mother...you have been my rock throughout this time of struggle. Mom, you are appreciated beyond the expression of words.

And to my children... Domuniek, Nautica, Xavier, Mikhi, and Damarco - I love you all.

And to my brothers...Jerry, AD RIP, Power, Mirak, Rashad, my love for y'all is real.

And to the mothers of my children... thank you for having patience with me when I was warring with myself. To the love of my life, my wife, Olivia. You are a true Proverbs 31 woman.

And to my sisters... Alniesa, Leslie, Nicole, Tia, and Sheena Ingram, RIP - like my love for my brothers, my love for y'all is real.

And to my editor Hamzah aka Snake Doc... thanks for helping me "Bounce" back-we did it, baby!

And to all my fallen comrades who died way too early...RIP: Denver Lane, Billy Shane, Bubbles (female), Bubbles (male), Brandon, Supreme, Dizzy, Cato (St. Paul Minnesota) Draper, Gunnz, Killer K, Dope Boy, Kay-Ree, Top, Lil'Boss, Hollywood, Bigz, Diamond, Will, Tammy, Jabba Jaws, Link, Turbo, Jay, Rink, Gunner, Soup, Danny Boy, Jabree, Kaliek, Markeem, Maniac, Keylow, Lil' Murda, Big J, Flip, Samson, Doe Boy, Bunk, Jessie, Tiff B, J-Roc, Type, Kayson, Taco, Teflon, Barry, Ram, T-Roc, Smitty, Marnie, Black Heat, Butch Kasidy, Black Seed, Dapa Don, Gee, S-God, Yas, Un-do, Ya Ya, Capon, Nino, Red Beard, Bullseye, Red Rum, Chuck Taylor, Kane, 4-Line, Tracy, Mo-Better, Da Da, Lucky, Pebbles, Stacy, Baby D, Jay (New Brunswick), T-Roc, Yam, Noodles, Black, 50 Cal, and Saun. Too many... too soon... all because of the addiction to gang-bangin'. Thank God I am now a Recovering Addict!

A special thanks to Chicago Interrupters. Keep fighting to save our brothers and sisters. Also, to the Ida B. Wells Projects in Chicago... all you chiefs out there-let's raise up and begin to live life. Watts-The Gardens-it's time to live life and allow our babies to grow up and become leaders of tomorrow. The D (Detroit). -East Side-What up, Doe! Let's rebuild the city!!!

And to all those individuals out there struggling with the addiction of gang-bangin'... remember, don't die dead!

About the Author

Dewan "Gullie Boy" Dennis no longer exists. Dewan Dennis, on the other hand, is spiritually reformed and is a "Recovering Addict". He holds a Doctorate degree in Divinity. In the meantime, in between time, Dewan continues to mentor inmates inside New Jersey State Prison on how to remove themselves from the "Death Style" of gang-bangin'. He has become a certified public speaker and Adult Education tutor-two things which he plans to use to further his message.

Presently, he is working on two more books, and he has completed a documentary that focuses on the discovery of PTSD in gang members.

Dewan worked closely with Jack Callaham, the Chair Emeritus of the Governor's Community Outreach Board. Together, they gave prisoners the opportunity to participate in the spiritually based program, Kenosis.

Mr. Dennis plans to tour the country while speaking to youths about the "death Style" of gang-bangin'. He is a licensed Minister who preaches and teaches the Gospel inside of New Jersey State Prison, using his testimony to further the Gospel.

CITIES THAT NEED US....

Newark, N.J., Camden, N.J., Patterson, N.J., Trenton, N.J., New Brunswick, N.J. Philadelphia, P.a. Chicago, Ill., Compton, Ca., Watts, Ca., Oakland, Ca., the entire Bay Area, Dallas, Tx. Inglewood, Ca. South Central L.A, Ca., Little Rock, Ark, Memphis, TN., Atlanta, Ga. Miami, Fl., Detroit, Mi., Nashville, TN., Charlotte, NC., New Port News, Va. Richmond, Va. Harlem, N.Y., Brooklyn, N.Y., Queens, N.Y., Bronx, N.Y. Birmingham, AL., Bishopville, Sc. Flint, Mi. , Saint Louis, Mo., New Orleans, La., Baton Rouge, La., Kansas City, Mo., Cleveland, OH. Gary, In., South Bend, In., ...**and so many other cities in which gang-banging has destroyed our communities.**

QUESTIONS FOR GROUP DISCUSSION

1. In the Dennis Report, do you believe if Raheem had been raised in a loving home, his life would have turned out differently?

2. In Chapter 1, "The Addiction," do you believe those individuals that are addicted to gang banging should be provided the same treatment that our war veterans are provided?

3. In Chapter 2, do you believe the relevant question is, why would someone Join a gang, or why would they stay?

4. In Chapter 3, did you notice how the author describes the double life that most gang bangers live? In your opinion, why is this so?

5. In Chapter 4, the author talks about Accountability. Do you believe everyone; the Teachers and Law Enforcement, should take Accountability for the conditions in our communities?

6. In Chapter 5, the Author addresses the gang culture and the violence that engulfs the lifestyle. Do you believe that the daily activity of the gang banger creates a dependence, which has the potential to lead to an addiction?

7. Chapter 6, "Gang Banging Mother" In your opinion, why is the addiction to gang banging so powerful and addictive that it will cause a mother to neglect her child?

8. In Chapter 7, the author talks about how the gang banger chases after a life that's not real. In your opinion, what are some of the reasons that someone would go to that extreme if what they're chasing after isn't real?

9. Chapter 8 talks about how trauma, such as PTSD, affects the gang banger. Do you believe those who have been diagnosed with this form of mental illness should have the findings presented in their pre-sentencing report for the court's consideration?

10. In Chapter 9, the author invites you to the pledge what are your thoughts about it?

11. In Chapter 10, The Cure. Do you believe the C.R.E.E.D. program should be turned into a curriculum for Jails, Prisons, Halfway Houses, High Schools, and Universities?

A Note
From the Author

Thank you for reading this book, I am humbled by the support. My fight to help eradicate the senseless violence that plagues our inner cities will never end. I know that with much prayer and hard work on a collective front, we can provide a haven for our at-risk youth.

I have been buried alive in New Jersey State prison for 19 years for a gang related crime I did not commit. The State of New Jersey charged and convicted me on three counts of murder by arson because of my former leadership position in the gang. Found guilty by association.

Visit my Instagram page @dewandennis to support the Justice for Dewan Dennis campaign. I am thankful for the love from all my supporters. As a result of your support, there are over 6,000 signatures on my petition. The battle continues... without you I can't finish it.

To learn more about my petition, visit: Change.org

JUSTICE FOR DEWAN

Once again, thank you for all the love. God bless!

Dewan Dennis

Don't miss out!

Visit the website below and you can sign up to receive emails whenever DEWAN DENNIS publishes a new book. There's no charge and no obligation.

https://books2read.com/r/B-A-YPFEB-NLBYC

BOOKS 2 READ

Connecting independent readers to independent writers.